COSMOS AND SPHERES

A FEW SELECTED POEMS FROM KRYSTAL VOLNEY THE POETESS

Order this book online at www.trafford.com
or email orders@trafford.com

Most Trafford titles are also available at major online book retailers.

Printed in the United States of America.

ISBN: 978-1-4669-0887-1 (sc)
ISBN: 978-1-4669-0886-4 (e)

Library of Congress Control Number: 2011962961

Trafford rev. 03/28/2012

 www.trafford.com

North America & international
toll-free: 1 888 232 4444 (USA & Canada)
phone: 250 383 6864 ♦ fax: 812 355 4082

TABLE OF CONTENTS

ACKNOWLEDGEMENTS

Her influences and muses have been Mozart, Van Gogh, Emily Dickinson and Claude Monet.

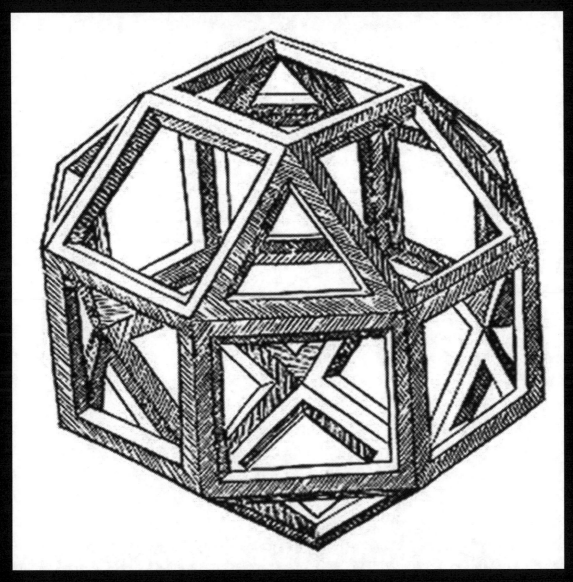

"Poetry is the music of the soul, and, above all, of great and feeling souls."- Voltaire

UNDERSTANDING COSMOS AND SPHERES

The title of the book has a lot to do with how people live their lives. Cosmos connotes the universe and everything that exists anywhere. It also defines an orderly or harmonious system. Spheres connote a particular environment or walk of life. Ever since I was younger, I've been fascinated with stars in the night sky and fell in love with the artistic piece 'Starry night' from pa inter Van Gogh. I compare the planets to human beings based on the description of each one from scientific research and also each planet as a sphere in the solar system. To me, the earth is somewhat like the solar system and different peoples like the planets in relation to the sun. This of course is not a spiritual or religious theory. However, I believe in God.

BIOGRAPHY OF POETESS

Krystal Victoria Gabrielle Volney.
Her interest in poetry started early, and as a child she often wrote short stories and songs as a hobby. Her favourite novels were the Nancy Drew files, the Babysitter's club and the famous five. The 21 year old poetess and playwright writes in categories such as fashion, romance, the environment and children's poetry. She views humans as both monarch and emperor butterflies because of the transformation from an egg into a butterfly showcasing the metamorphosis as various stages of one's experiences throughout life. Her analysis states that as a result of the prodigious difference between each human being in the global society, experiences differ and some persons mature into butterflies while some remain at a particular stage permanently at various points in their longevity. The contemporary poetess's character is floral. In the 21st century, this m eant that one consisted of many petals and each petal told a different story of who she was. She saw lily and hibiscus flowers as demonstrating what it meant to be a woman and a lady.

VEUX- TU M'EPOUSER

"Для каждой любви есть сердце где-то на его получение"

How long will ye make one wait in Kolomenskoye?
It is my unyielding heart that hath awaited four years for this hour.
It is thy love and our truth that brought us together.
The mood is silent and the clock had finished ticking its lazy eye.
Its slow ticking was torment to my element.
In my heart thy name rests and shall I wait as long as a lifetime.

The essence of waiting is not a f orbidden thing.
It is waiting in vain for thy courtship.
Love putteth and honoureth.
It sweareth.
It changeth not f or its own hurt and speaketh the truth in its heart.
Ye has given it a sign and strings of an instrument to play.

O how one yens to live vicissitudes without fear.
The reverie and penchants of a nobleman with a benign butterfly who does not wish to flutter here.
The spasm of my spirit and a ticker filled with amorousness in
it. An oculus for enchantment and the lovesome lie of a lover.
Does one rather an oligarch as a honcho with a f eathered wing?
An eagle that prays over the cadaver of his bride with a salvaged
ring. Thy sunken pride that his pruriency dwells with a handful of
mothers.

Ye honey'd smile that speaketh for early spring's beautiful blooming roses from
Genoa. W hy I'd paint a portrait of thy dovelike face and capture thy scent in a perfume
bottle. Inhaling the fresh air that I see on a nebulous winter Yuletide eve in this far
away land. For what I cannot bestow is the resplendent chopard blue that lays in his
hand.
Never say nay another time, my flittering butterfly, for I am both charming and kind.
And with a stronger arm against thy chaste breast and into thy eyes are holy glimmers of thoughts one dare not express.

I'd take you into a secret garden of powder snow and I'd fight Narcissus while skating to and
fro. And steep'd the frigid winter skies with a twirl and a dance of Andalusian flamenco.
Chill'd by thy comeliness and o'er the bridge through the church gates we go,
Down on my knee I am, holding thy delicate hand with sanctuary lamps and candles lit in the
background. The stars shout to the heavens and before the throne of God I ask f or thy life with me
And momentous tears dripp'd into thy palm as I seek'd my companion for where thy silence dwells, I desire wedding bells.

Ye as my wife, against that phantom amidst the shades of night with blood stain'd on his garment
His pale jealous glare with a Bubo scandiacus on his shoulder stood listening unaware of thy struggle with his chain of harlots
Into a silent room we ran and into a lunatic's paradise where soldiers were weak and as dumb as door knobs
W hat I intend is to embrace thy angelic face with kisses under the moonlight and have the gentle zephyrs tug thy hair of
curly carrots.
W andering into a lover's land and rap-a tap tap go my feet for I can see a picture of you and within the f og, mist and
clouds. Ye blushing lady with virtue and modesty adorn'd on thy white dress and at a distance a burning light e'er so
bright.
But I humbly await thy decision and hopes of joy to diffuse o'er my soul and into a ship we jump at the gentlewoman's request .

Our hearts alike both captured by fright and into this night of white,
Leaps into an Arctic world and to the North Pole where we freeze in love along with zooplankton and phytoplankton
And there we see the Chukchi, Evenks and some Koryaks with open arms under the Rigil Kentaurus sight
Camelopardalis, Corona Australis, Beta Ursae Minoris on this starry night caught in frostbite
I do wonder how we shall escape but swifter than the speed of sound, our allies take us where their homes are found
Snowmobiles and reindeers carry us to a heavenly place in this icy land where I take agai n thy hand
I give thee my sweet diamond dust, emerald ice and all from the biosphere that I can.

Take this kiss unto thy lips and feel strokes of burning desire as a thousand whips
All that we see are snowflakes flying as fireflies and with deep sighs
Breaths of frozen air standing amidst the roaring winds of Russian pins
Closing our eyes lock'd dreaming of another place where we could survive
W ith a tighter grasp our hands crack and suddenly came fighters from a
hive
Killer bees with hatred in their minds and teardrops down thy eyes in denial of these lies,

To the cherubims I cry to save my companion from this misery mourning
Thy cries pierce my heart as a dagger in the Battle of Sitka
W here there's weakness my patellas give in and my shame lays me in the morning
Unto the ice I lay alone left to die while enormous clouds cover me in the needle snow
But there stood Arphugitonos at the end of the world ready to take me into a transcendental realm

Controls of the wind lock'd me unto the ice where I s aw images of morbid fear
A reflection of bloodshed eternally nail'd in a picture of my lost dear
I curse the existence of her name from the depths of the earth I breathe one's last
One child would she bear to her king in between two lovers her heart is tor n.
Pericardiums in our phalanges and back to Rublyovka she is gone.

The spirit of the flame burneth from afar while faith kept me alive
Faithful love and a flight of sacred doves flew in to give me a sign.
Had I been so blind? The lady never said goodbye.
Knowing my heart's weakness with weather too gelid to think
Adorned in frost, departing the earth with Kerubiel and scorching bolts
Reclined in celestial eternity singing an aria of felicity
Falling into God's arms with a wreath of quietude and ecstasy.

Immortal and softened forevermore into the Almighty's zone
A colourful rainbow smile and a Being worthwhile in the afterlif e as his child
Far above the cirrus clouds o'er the buttermilk sky, I slept in the nebula in the pillars of creation
Floating in magnetic fields stuck in a dream in stellar evolution
Spirits of divinity cuddled my soul and took me to the omega nebula at His last supper
And scared at the sight, there sat Bartholomew, James and Andrew in an angelic light
The Lord's ivory eyes of lightning struck as I fell into a deeper dream
Imprinted kisses on my cheeks in endless time and tears of happiness fell as waterf alls unto the earth.

A new earth of rebirth where demons had been condemn'd to hell
No weeping and a broad highway of forsythias, cyclamen and Canterbury bells.
A large garden of Eden without serpents and a coruscating lake of trumpeter swans
Together they f orm'd a heart in this sublunary sphere singing a chiliad of dawns
Cherishing moments of transcendence and communion in a society that wished each other well.

THOUGHTS IN A MINOR

"Lernen Sie von gestern, lebe für heute, für morgen hoffen.
Das Wichtigste ist, nicht aufhört zu fragen"

W here do thy visions ruminate whilst eating pears in Uzbekistan,
when running one's fingers down the achromatic keys in Serbia.
Ye sprinter of longitude, thy wistful lullaby is sung from the icecaps on Greenland;
Caught up with the begrudgement of yesterday.

Populaces of people disappointed thy lonely willing heart,
And ye had contemplations of departing from a shuttle after falling apart.
Yet I gave you my support with thy past sentence of depression,
And for thee I pray to live a better way.

One squanders each finger, fulminating each memoir.
Onward with progress. Profanation is f orbidden.
Lost is meant to be found.
Thus thy transudation authenticates a revolutionary day.
Mourns the woman of a broken heart filled with abhorrence and no swain who dared stay.
And from door to door she'd beg for their affection beneath her black veil,
W here there was no significant other where every man had play'd.

To her I give my best regards and hold her dear in noon felt
air,
W hile playing her naturals so white.
Offspring spend their generation hearkening in delight.
Hachikos examine everything concussing a
smile. Trajectory verbalizes all.

Waste not time listening to eighty-eight keys that sit to watch you play.
They desire to see ye snivel along with the sweat.
Never let their colours break thy posture.
Naturals and flats keep thy stature and forget their evil bet.
Since to you my friend, who hast thou to choose which path she takes
To gain his love is a never-ending feat,
And thy expectations of his being he shall never meet.

Let's depart the earth together and follow the league of the stars
Into a dreamer's land to Alpha Centauri and Epsilon Eridani
To Jupiter Jungle and Saturn's ring while dancing,
Steps of merriment and liberty, forgetting about insanity
The music of the moon with its satellite eyes on us
For intervals and f or hours, jumping from sphere to sphere

Follow my lead as we dodge shooting comets like ruger bullets,
Release the trouble from thy anima, holding bouquets of
Hydrangeas.
Gathering asterisms in thy pockets and dismiss the foster father fear.
A mighty nebula is in our path and electromagnetic radiation is near
W ith courage we shall move on and to return to a dangerous world,
In solitude as mangrove branches with strengths of cosmos untold.

Shall we take this sway and swing with our ruthless roots in the ground?
W ho dare come our way in this planet of luminosity with Aegea holding a crown.
Dauntlessness and tenacity in an elliptical galaxy listening to an angel's song.
Accompanied by electromagnetic waves from Celtic harps that played for long.
Shocked with ebullience from a group of Electrophori electricus while laying down.

Oh and ourselves like children, pure and masterful never looking back at the past
Knowing our worth, forgetting the tiresome hurt and that hath been said
There's power in our wildest screams in ceaseless fanciful dreams, and our yearnings fed
Neglected and affected, some bruised ones that suffered long
Giving thyself and those that wept bitterly for the men who justified their wrong.

Thy romance lasted in the moment and to the floor one ululated, holding one's head
And hopes in the lioness's den and prayers nocturnally while laying in bed.
Let go of the detrimental anamnesises from ancient times
Chagrined and f earful of being with other gentlemen of different kinds

Contemptuous and misanthropic, ne'er give up on being optimistic
Ne'er hold thy breath or pity thyself in endless darks, stained with love marks
Prithee, my sisters with polar hearts wagging castigating fingers like tungsten darts

So shalt thou release the chains of mental blockage,
While he strokes the keys on thy piano staring at thee in thy eyes
Emotional pusillanimity being thy extreme enemy, mistrusting saying a dozen goodbyes.
But hold steadily my treasured friend whilst laying,
In a pippin field with moist fingers feeling the wind gazing
Accept this proposal as a recherché unicorn queen with a spirit so keen

'Tis an enchanting sight in the most sacrosanct sense
To see thrilling physiognomies as the ladies wear chandelier gowns
Ah, with necks outstretched as Cygnus columbianus sitting on lawns
Nether parasols tigresses are settled and dwelleth with old nerves as tense
By the new standards of a pulchritudinous butterfly in lambent territory.

YOU'VE SOLD FASHION

W hat did fashion declare yesterday?
Fabric flaunted on the mannequins, floribunda and flirtation.
Cosmos with couturiers, cover girls, negligees, exotic swim wear dwelling in a global nation.
Canadian corsets, Juliette sleeves, haute couture from Paris, New York City, Hong Kong and Milano.
The legend has begun.
A fashion contessa's curtsey meets a gentleman's gleam. Bow and arrow.
One never gave up through the arduous times.
W hither not whilst letting thoughts of faddism settle, sipping Pétrus and Romanée-Conti wine.

Work thy flair zenith, you've sold f ashion.
Could my eyesight be blown away by this vogue passion?
This discovery gave way to knowledge.
The solar telescope mastered authority as one thrived.
W ith accelerating motion presenting each collection at every season.
So may I, holding Provence rose petals scatter them in every region.

In silence they rest, collecting treasures and one hath sold fashion.
Don't exit until you've bared it all.
Murmurs of appreciation and flows of panoply as in a magnificent
ball. You've sold fashion.
Ah me! Now wheref ore the crowd sat in mirth approving of the designer's call.
Spectrum lights, incandescent flashes and colour temperature on the catwalk stages.

The thread and Bernina conquered every art of armscying, tailoring and zippering that there was to
conquer. The scissors tangoed with every line that the stylograph wrote as the fashion houses applauded in
thunder. Fashion is sold. The couturier did not wish to stop designing.
W ho had known! The poet continued writing.
„Twas worth the while at every opportunity with frolicsome guests in these tiresome quests.

The fashioners brought their houses down.
Ere I had heard on this fantasy terrene it took many sketches and fittings of gowns
Paisley shawls, waistcoats and neckties as the couturiers slaved overtime with many frowns
And then the final hour came with a gentle breeze from the West Indies.
The clothes and the cadenza danced under the moon's effulgence.
The models and supermodels silhouetted as coryphées down the ramp.
W hen the show was finally over the earth covereth with a large Magellanic cloud
The after party began at midnight hour where invitees were greeted with cherry blossom flowers.

So might I say, with a little longer to stay with handfuls of black eyed Susans and showers of Asteraceae
Much to converse coupled with a reflective image to my heart and a lovely mystery
solved. I listened to Tchaikovsky play with light spirits and lemons in a nutcracker suite,
As the sunrise came in the aurora with lasers of
heat. You've sold fashion.

TOKYO TOUCHDOWN

Ah dash! The bullet bolt'd with the sonance of a pistol in Helsinki.
The aircraft landed after hours of gliding o'er the boundless cerulean skies.
All the cosmos smiled at the greatest race of the century as the scorching sun rose.
Tiger Lily airlines had sponsor'd the match in memory of the W right Brothers.
The other engines were not orchestrated as their Naphtha continued dripping and the men froze.
It was not their immediate destiny to fly, higher than a glider kite,
O so high and they wondered why.

One said- when racing against time to the lovely gleams of light,
That they thought they could, should and ultimately they would.
Alas! Their little planes finally departed and expeditiously made the touchdown negating the spite.
Tok-yo touchdown.

Two flying machines stopped in grave and imminent danger halfway,
W ith no power calling 'Mayday, Mayday Mayday'
At once, but the others far-flung o'er Mount Kumotori had nothing to worry,
Eclipse Spyders sped on the roads at the viewing in a hurry.

Surely someone cried above the traveller's head,
For the rivalry was perceptible as the first plane had already arrived there.
Beneath the sun, who told the time that these airplanes took from the pioneers of powered
flight? Sudden glimpses at the smashing appearance for their parents,
Like a day of Cursus and Quinquertium in Olympia,
But one ought not f ear throughout the fight.

The red and white colours of Tokyo show'd on the faces of the medals.
W alks to the stage in the most delightful manner as one's mind was settled
Clapping in standing ovation, the women were in tears at their victory in history.
The winner train'd as a champion trains in a battle of the
fittest. That was the man's word to the press.
The bugles echoed in their tender ears leaving the losers depressed.

THE BEAUTY

Beauty stared proudly at her reflection in the vermeil mirror,
while her golden cup held a mixed glass of Perrier and Tasmanian rain.
Spoke the mirror to her in a fervent dream –„Wake up from your egocentricity!"
O how the tears of fizzing water splashed in her face as the beast Narcissus deemed her vain and stained.
Great beauty smiled sublimely as she adorned her neck with Akoya and Kasumiga Pearls in a graceful way.
For hours she stared at her appearance analyzing it until the sunlight came, rustling the leaves at the break of day.
Smitten by her image, it became a display of bride and bridegroom stuck in her romance of mental dimensions.
Nightingales sang and cinnamon scops owls hooted at sunrise to the mystery of the opera singer.
Beauty smelt her centif olia and grandiflora roses, snapping her sharpened fingers.
„Tis an evident axiom that true beauty ought to come from within.
The melodist blew velvety kisses to the mirror with soft innocent smiles,
as the vainglorious beast agreed to her actions while cachinnating at this mistaken child.
So lively her f ace lit up at her reflection of f acial symmetry and Koeslag"s koinophilia.
How glorious is this vision and the humour of a beauty?
Pleasure she gained watching old canvases of her
Youth.
The lady brought this art making comparisons before the mirror displaying the truth.
The Great Finsteraarhorn and Schreckhorn waved at her human age as her divine winsomeness faded with time.
But by a Scottish philosopher's word, in the mind one is truly beautiful within.
If certain, „tis contradictory to her as the Beauty"s contemptuous interior said otherwise.
This colloquy about 'beauty' taught Narcissus the beast as her haughty words showed her superficiality.
For by worldly standards, the woman's exterior had been aged and ugly.
Ah! The complex gift of beauty declared not to trust his true reflection as it may deceive him.
Of self- love and perception, she protected her image as beauty had been in the eye of the
beholder. W hat immortality existed in the thoughts for the flushing blood of this lady,
W here heavenly bodies lied before her archangelic wing.
Twinkles of light entered Rayonnant rose windows as in the Notre de Paris.
Knowing her shadow's image in a pool of water, sternly she questioned her beauty once again
O dame! Trembling woman wrapped up in a paranoid fixation on perfection and mathematics with the eyes of Pythagoras before a group of imaginary men.
The relieved sigh of a classical beauty with style and fashion from Renaissance Europe where the sun was most torrid!
May it be a gentlewoman's charisma, elegance, confidence, intelligence or personality?
W herever she existed in the society she lived, defining the sensational woman called
beauty.

THE FLOWER

Flower so bright,
flower so new.
W hy does the humming bother you?
Spending your time, wishing you knew.
Speak with honour.
Stand with dignity.

Suppose the humming stopped humming,
what say you?
Trees look down on you and say nothing.
Let your nectar stay sweet and let the sun delight in your fashion.

The wind blows alone but it feels your presence.
Its spirit feels the fluster of your petals.
Trying to grasp onto one. Just one.
Till it realizes that you stand firm.

Your leaves whisper sweet nothings,
proclaiming your fun and varying colour.
Pretty with no inside jollifies the leaves when falling down.
Don't let whispers tell your time f or they too want to see you f all.

The branches watch everything with intentions of mocking
you. They too want to see everything falling, leaves and all.
They see it fit to stand out in front of everything.
W hen the rain falls, they laugh to see you drained.
They dry faster more than anything.
But don't wilt flower. I.
Flowers are meant to stay beautiful.

UGLY RUTHLESS BRANCHES MOCKING THE FLOWER BECAUSE FLOWERS ARE PRESENT EVERYWHERE.

TWO- FACED LEAVES WITH LINES (SWEET NOTHINGS)

PARIS'S PEARLS

O it was an extraordinary item f or a dignified belle.
Her muse was grace. The city of romance and tales.
Belle was enthralled by this necklace of outstanding worth.
Pearls which classified her as a perfect score.
Monarch butterflies roamed in the Rosa glauca gardens as the ladies danced to Ars Nova with men on the floor.

Their parasols twirled behind their heads as they swayed as vaned feathers.
Paris's pearls were extracted from the Pinctada maxima on the coast of the sea.
For how Belle's plea tasted the kiwi fruit of the bloom as she broke down crying in her state of doom and self-pity.
Day had become night. The Eiffel tour brought new memories to her life.
Her love lost was her French desire.
The necklace was her obsession as it called wonders to her flair.
Diamonds are forever but pearls are also everlasting.
Belle resisted her French f ascination as she left Paris behind with closed doors.

A curious witness glanced at her body that veered and gazed into the sublime f orenoon
sky, with tears of torture and pangs of grief.
Curious I overheard vociferations along with my curious eye,
of her aesthetics demanding a sign of solace in the midsummer's heat.

A puissant light scintillated with rays as effulgent,
so bright as the blade of a sword and the cry of a knight,
unto the sunflowers in Swiss meadows and fields.
But by Great Leonardo's view, her insecurity could not beat fair Mona Lisa's smile,
for without jewels she still had style.

The hyperborean winds blew into the twilight.
O night, where have the stars been?
For Saturn with its ring is most beautiful in the Macrocosm said the sherry and gin.
How the planets aligned at the apperception of belle in between heaven and hell!

She fell into a deep rest in the region of Haute-Savoie beneath Mont Blanc
W here the grey daylight's nimbostrati finally came with light snow
Covered with a cloak crying in desolation and calamity over her lost pearls.
O agony! O misery and how she reiterates her sobbing f or this treasure her heart deemed best.

Can this despondent grisette with her earthly tongue tell what no mortal ever
knew? Laying throughout the snow flurries as a nutter where little breezes blew
Her quest f or love where fellows tore her apart when she gave up everything from the start.
Listening thunder rolled and the mountain resigned at Belle's lost of hope
And there, she threw herself at willing men where there was no one to help her cope.

Behold, she woke up in another land,
Inside Egyptian sheets in the pyramid of Kufu holding a Pharaoh's hand
Gleamed at hieroglyphics with her name and on a golden pillow sat her pearl
chain. From the urges of her frenzy, shadows and dimmed lights
Duties and charms fit for cobras engaging in fights

To choose a path and run away from this new home like a chamber slave
Through the gates of drought and wind, battling sandstorms f orming a wave
Yet she grabs her pearls and runs like a domesticated W uzhishan pig
Look thou to the horizon and take thy bliss with thee as holding an oil rig
Fashion'd by the sunshine her jewels fell burying in the sand
W ith thy own ridicule she pant'd screaming regarding herself as a fool.

Bag of bones shook in another place in a different time
Trauma and concussion in a hospital bed with breathless hours
Ensanguined and hallucinations of spirits with glasses of wine
W here are the pearls? Soothing memory with some lady mantle and lisianthus flowers.
A wooden cross placed to her head to exorcise her boundless mind.

ADMONITION TO FLORAL COMBATIVENESS

To my Amorphophallus titanum wounded from the cosmos's chemical assassin
with thy floral cadaver, in faith I stare at thee with harmonious lullabies
W hich honoureth thy carrion flower with the enshrined Prussian citizenship under the f atalistic skies
Together we escape, you and I from the Sumatran tribes off to the Botanic tournament to win.
The zephyrs sang ethereal arias to the flittering Orphic butterlies in a poetic atmosphere,
Parasol-shaded as fanciful leaders to the cavalcades as the twilight drew near.

To battle in the Swedish Pomeranian conservatory and hither come algorithmic decisions from fictional humanoids
W insome musical cadences from the air's melodramatic orchestras of contrabassoons and classical
piccolo for gains of sporadic blooms on the eminent night of judgement competing against pulchritudinous
foes. Thou, o amorphophallus titanum art the f airest of them flowery all,
Beside wooden cages of obsequious Half-moon Conures bef ore the shadowy existence of Odysseus
To thy inflorescent sight a midnight umbra came with his Tibetan Sand Fox's cunning intelligence.

Dare I stare at the Malaysian Rafflesia arnoldii in its lonesomeness and cumbersome rarity?
Unisexual and in its proximity with a stigma were throngs of homunculi with cogitations of Jung's alchemy.
Lightning bugs in their lowly kind, dined in assemblages of Rafflesia cabbages tuned into the poetic
rhyme. Deepest condolences to thee in thy endangered state,
W ith pitied reactions of fetid smells attracting Scorpionflies to pollinate.
And to ye, my competitive enemy in the defense of the Amorphophallus titanum,
W ith Einstein' s philosophy of passionate curiosity, why should anyone honour
thee?

Macaque monkeys as noisy schoolboys beat seven-spotted ladybug formations of Sri Lankan drums
Seated in the apex of a Birch tree's crown in a screeching spectacle of delight.
Away I go, with contemptuous intent of thy corpse, applauding a strange time in this fight.
W eaving widow spiders approach not here in globules of thickened nebulous air on this eerie March night
Did thee stutter? Did ye hesitate? Do I dare speculate? Back to Borneo thou shall return to thy fizzling f ate.
And before it's too late, to a moonlight's sonata on a requiem date to dance with death, thy
mate. Bef ore it's too late. Bef ore it's too late.

Among a group of **Spur-Throated** grasshoppers snickering on carnivorous pillows,
Discussing herbaceous politics, ensconced Lady Dionaea muscipula in the crisis beneath the weary willows
Supposedly, in the ambuscading of prey with esteemed Mimosa and Bladderworts,
Torturing the eyes of the innocent few, so delicately mocked and egocentrically hurt
O parsimonious Narcissus, do we wrestle phrases and exchange vows?
Forlorn hope f or thee while overturning a lingzhi mushroom to administer thy health
Cheers to thine deadly charm and to thee, awaits a requiem date to dance with death, thy
mate. Back to thy rapacious dominion. Before it's too late. Before it's too late.

THE STEELPAN

Salutations to Trinidad and T obago!
We're here with our suitcases sitting below the silver stars at night on a Domingo
And this is where islanders play, all throughout the dimmet and during the day.
The euphonic steelpan is a melody that presents itself as the bevy's culture.
Coruscations of dancing shadows come together as bright lights flicker on the f aces of the gay.

Each part of the tenor, cello, bass and Quadrophonic
Formulate a glorious puzzle,
that the pan sticks impetuously hit anticipating to unravel.
The orchestras amalgamate playing a mesmerizing song.
The earth had stopped moving to a sight so impressing,
As the gravity bounced the spirits of the people into the air along with their costume wear.

They battle in fury against each other amidst twilight in town.
The trinbagonians career in their own fashion with their spoons and bottles.
Both young and senescent cheer on concurrently in perspiration with
towels.
The Queen's park savannah is where it all goes
down,
or they actuate it on the boulevards while promenading to the st eelpan
sound.

Conviction in the repertoire as the calypsonians vocalize musical renditions of
Kaiso.
The pannists drumming in theatrical perf ormances during the
Panorama.
From the evolution of pan, they stroke Tamboo-Bamboos like stonemason
Hammers.
O national instrument of Trinidad and T obago, so greatly loved all o'er the
world.

And as far as the imagination goes and where the light wind blows,
Striped like an Equus burchellii the season of steelpan ne'er
Changes,
as the boom of the thunder roars in its yard o'er the horizon while chop sticks tap on the
steel. Tell that to the creatures that live far away as we hop on a plane after a week and
leave.

Always we visit in Spring every year and with reasons of
holiday
Might fancy the island with dancing tourists, and our muscles they
move
To the jouncing and skipping in Port-of- Spain, maddened by the mood with nothing to
prove
And oh! Photographs and videotapes of memories we keep, while thinking of the fiesta as we
weep.

THE HIBISCUS

Hibiscus so extraordinary, your nature sprinkles sparkle.
Each petal draws a new attraction to the viewer.
Your scent brings revelation of love, passion and poise.
Your cosmic colour vocalizes answers of blossoming grace.

The flower exhales oxygen of fashion unknown to breath.
Its sepals symbolize a guardian protecting her valor.
Breathe hibiscus, the world is watching. You have attracted its attention.

Your pistil is loaded with beauty. Your style stabilizes its stamen.
Pretty knows your name. It keeps its eye on you. You've made a new best friend.
Your ovaries multiply your fame and glamour is your energy.
The world is your magnifying glass expanding your storage.
Your dress is twirling clockwise as age seems to have added more taste t o you.

Sweet hibiscus, you are the center of contemplation in the Mallow family
Hibiscus cannabinus, Hibiscus sabdariffa, Hibiscus syriacus, Hibiscus rosa-sinensis
The trumpet petals blow along with the flute pistil as an andante in a Mozart tune.
There's no other beauty in the sphere of Magnoliophyta that can outdo what the hibiscus can do.
Her inward beauty is highlighted as at the top of Mount Kosciuszko and a Darjeeling tea party at noon.

I have a hibiscus garden and I named it 'Le jardin des merveilles'
And in this place are Lapis Lazuli, Tigers eye and Amethyst gemstones where my lovely hibiscus has found its home and
well, She is sure to stay f orever young as she represents an allnatt diamond and the heart of eternity.
Her classical antiquity stems as f ar as the quiet f ormation of the earth and one enjoys her tranquility.

Heaven and earth gape at her mystery caught in the Hibisceae, attracting butterflies and
Bees.
Each outcry of the Malvoideae to the rising sun at a sight on the shores of the Caribbean Sea
Shall never be another flower I lay my eyes on and repeats to thee thy grand beauty
A truth that's told with a floret who sits so sly whose philosophy displayed a splendid key

Every night and every morn' I acknowledge her charm and some are led to believe a lie
But my musical hibiscus with a f aithful eye, genuine as can be exhibiting honesty
To those who dwell in Tahiti, the fruits of tradition for marriage and her availability
O gumamela, fill my life with joy and let divine raindrops gather on her petals when the air laughs in gleeful wit
Come into my hand and dance a blue Danube waltz on an evening dedicated to Strauss.

W oody shrubs and Polynesian hibiscus fibres worn as grass skirts as well as wigs
In my hand analyzing its expertise and artistry
Is it possible that such a beautiful flower which produces lovely tea
-Cranberry, Raspberry and Blueberry possesses such gentility?

Emerging from buds, two battling for the sport of classical
fencing Pistils slashing and swinging like Radaelli against Nadi in
a fight As a Medieval Queen Hibiscus dubbing a knight,
W ith her father's pistil sword at the sight.

Then said, arise Sir Tiliaceus with thy bright yellow petals
Limestone background in addition to his acidic temperament
And fancies the f our movements of sonata, andante and scherzo
From a blast of Beethoven ending in an attacca as all is settled.

SCARLET IBIS

There's no other bird more TRANSCENDENT than the Scarlet Ibis,
as her skeletal arms uncover her ardour with vivid, ruby feathers.
She captur'd the show with her eminent bald eagle in the Caroni Swamp with luminous weather.
The creature demands being photographed between the Mangroves but acknowledges no autographs.
The fever of the bird is contagious in her noonday image and with a sugarplum head laying in her brackish bed.

The island of Trinidad is abounding with umpteen ornamented birds.
The broken branches work as slides for play and when all the clouds are grey as the weathermen say.
These scarlets in marshlands whose best friends are humming and birds of paradise that convey many
cynosures. But don't disdain the rufous-tailed cocrico. He sniggers at his rubicund kinsperson as their beaks vie in
thunder.
I gasp'd f or air at the sight on the hills of Trinity f or together they aspir'd and they achiev'd.
To succeed as Columbus did upon his distressing voyage of Santa Maria and what it represent'd, Mister Ibis once wonder'd.

The Scarlet Ibis is the envy of the bird megacosm as her nature is natural.
She esteems leeway in tidal lagoons as her exhibition requires perpetual
attention. Trinidad, Venezuela and Brazil fancy her demeanour due to her beauty
and stride.
The forests command respect for her comportment in Trinidad as she is the national pride.

There may be a silver stream with scarlets all inflam'd by summertide's blazing rays where skies are clear,
cheering each other while splashing in the black water f orgiving the sad murmur of the roots that sit and
stare. From the shadowy claws of those telescope eyes where anaconda snakes lie wrapped around the
branchlets
Melting to the splendour of these creatures and in the beauty of the morning one mock'd the danger of their
strength. W ho better to stand on this sturdy branch than Mister Scarlet Ibis with a hard back of glory and swampy
scent?

Farewell my friend as tears filled thy eyes as my canoe moved away,
Does the winged bird fear a swampland without spectators that left for
the day?
And he holds my bag of food with greed, never turning his face,
Seeking to drive the boat crazy by hovering above the people with
haste.

THE GREAT BOOT

The Malachite Boot is observed by multitudes, visiting her quay.
It has carried many brigantines of globetrotters and newcomers from abroad.
She fathoms and anticipates no other being greater than omnipotent God.
O Maafa! W hose heart that hath pain f or the Ashanti of Ghana,
And the Yoruba of Nigeria brought on the slaveships to the home island.
W hat foolish agony f ell on the backs of the tugged blacks,
 And whips for days to the East Indians wailing for the love of Fatel Rozack.

My purring Burmilla gleams at the sight of premium tuna while fitting his great boot on.
Smiling back at him admiringly, stroking his wretch'd but spoil'd hair as I continue noting down.
The colours under the sun coruscate daily on the skins of the Spaniard, French Creole, Portuguese, and mixed people.
Prosperous, pitiable, ebony, white, red, yellow, brown.
Businesses, oil refineries, f ashion mansions and the man about town.
Saying, 'History tells the story of time',
And pitying the trials faced by its people whilst exploring the mind.

Choirs across the land hum like a Scandinavian Gregorian chant. Thou
flummoxed me and moved me so, many cultures and folklores Santa
Maria, El Correo and La Vaquenos brought by Cristoforo Colombo
W earing his cape to the future sounds of Chacón, Abercromby and Sedeño
It noshes at thy soul to see the nation's struggles of the past
Picking Aloysia triphylla from a group of Verbenaceae covered with yellow jacket wasps

Despite the crime and the evils that roam the land with no time to
discuss, the people are embracing, cheerful and they magnetize smiles.
Conch shells, starfish, lavalier, inexpressible discoveries and many are surprised.
If there is one patria in the galaxy one should go,
do sojourn in the twin island republic of Trinidad and Tobago.

HEIGHTS

Altudinous! Higher than high flagellates such trouble!
A dominion where no man dared to go.
He schlepps with the wind but his afflictions held him down.
The nutcrackers dangled their wings in the distance in Marrakech,
whistling welcoming chorales.
So sing a song to heaven my ethereal Erithacus rubecula to eradicate my melancholy sentiments.

His highness saunter'd the bridge of heights.
Courage was his accomplice; his eminence never walk'd away from trouble.
Trouble gave new meaning to his life. A new adventure.
His stunts postulated flying and many watch'd on in fear of his wailing.
Does dust settle where the wind blows? He was a privateer in no man's land.
New worlds to acquire while leaping as a snow leopard against the thought of failing.

His purpose was to conquer this Swiss mountain of Monte Rosa overshadowing him.
Dynamite was the size of his fingers, facing this height.
His highness broke all barriers, surpassing the height of heights.
Hardships no longer existed.
He called it a day. The caper of all capers.
The acme gave him height, along with his ego.
His ego was his bride.
But fright and fear could not hold him back or lost in calm silence to overcome his supercilious pride.

THE BUTTERFLY KISS

W here do the Danaus plexippus and Papilio Ulysses fly when none flatter them?
Their wings flutter in Lithuania where the zephyr blows them.
Does anyone know the temperament of the butterfly?
His endearment blew them away.
They never knew his makeup.

Grandeur was never on his agenda. His genesis started off as an egg.
The burdensome experience. Smog. There were no availing hands.
The butterfly fluttered down memory lane in Tham Khao W ong land, simpering at the past.
The mighty ages of this creature cry on earth's doorstep on the exotic poinsettias in foreign lands.

And now alongside the hibiscus arnottianus immaculatus, fluttered a monarch
butterfly Tenderness while sleeping in her interior cup as the stars lended their eyes
like a spy Amongst the children of the globe in Nuremburg,
Camping in the timberland holding bottles catching Photuris fireflies;
Bioluminescence led the species that settled on the bark of the trees

His kisses were engineered by the nature and the time of his trials.
W herever he went, he gave not one harangue. His euphoria trusted in the Amazon
environment. The orchids and irises hiccupped at the butterfly kiss as he flittered his wings.
That was the sonority of their trumpets. Some things never change.
For many a wise man say when my friends came and few they were knocking at m y door,
and a butterfly that took the floor with deeds of kindness and what more were these caterpillars looking for?

A butterfly kiss like a grandmother's round face and a choco rose cake.
I saw a tiger lily and Roses of Sharon with a large cluster of Lycaenidae in a fragrant zone,
Inside the hazy rainforest where an emperor butterfly f ell in love with his equal upon the floral lake.
Kisses on their winged- cheeks were sweeter than a Käsekuchen cake that took overnight to
bake.
Let passions lay and laughter sound bring fresh showers of rainfall
down, On the fake leaves of chlorophyll f or the butterfly's sake.

LOVELY

O how lovely adores her name.
She beams at those who feel her nectarous inspiration.
She smothers her frizzies in honey,
revealing her intuition.
Much pleasure to the simple spirit of this stunning lass lightly wear ing her crown.

Lovely cognizeth a few and how great the amplitude of flowerets
that wish"d her well.
They utter pronouncements in Shanghai about her as far as love goes.
There is no distraction to her loveliness and oriental fashion.
Lovely wears a dress of splashed colour and sparkle.
Her f avourite is not displayed as far as lovely goes.
Hush all to hear the beating heart of this lovely lady with many coveting foes.

Lovely wanders only where her victims lay.
Is it a world of heartless men with not one to defend their dignity and say nay?
She never loses her game of flirtatious love.
There's a weeping willow that never once said hello to the perplexed dove.
But shalom watches this fellow with love.

Lovely leads smooth down the highway, leaning into the Almighty's
side because highways were made for love.
Grace winks at lovely because elegance is her middle name.
Poise guffaws as its her family member.
Lovely momentarily claps as her f ashion show has finished.

Dear dame, in this province of exquisiteness
Arise out of thy effervescence from fantasies of Zinfandel and Gewürztraminer
O sublunary world, what shall one do without thee?
I harmonize an alluring melodia at lengths in a lovely season feeling free
Carefree joys and instruments of love spinning under the Supernovae
Speed of light in the celestial sphere with closed eyes following the dreamer's way.

THE BOHEMIAN HIPPIE

O gentlewoman whose sobriquet was Bonny!
She was a bohemian hippie from Melbourne who rode a Brumby
with chartreuse vellum and a stylograph.
In the dawn of day the golden sun that shines o'er her head dazzled
 in her peacock eyes that visualized a honeyed surprise.
Bonny's chignon was comely, stramineous and delicate with starfish clips.
Her alter-ego was a polychromatic flowered pubescent with flair who often swayed her hips.

Her peasant skirt was voguish and ecru with concord sign prints.
In her psychedelic roseate purse she kept a packet of Australian Perth mints.
Bonny's jewellery was tribal, aurulent and pink, displaying her style.
Like Madame Valpin with Chrysanthemums and Van Gogh with Irises,
Bonny's simplicity was her sophistic ation and it was worth the while.

A Candied apple luxury carriage that her brumby pulled,
Took her to a traveller's land away from cricket monsters,
expanding her life span.
Her soul in agony trying to hold the faith of her tired horse's smile.
Take this, a troop of Macropus fuliginosus that led the track in Queensland.

She ensconced near a fountain with an Argentine toco toucan
And a Crimson Rosella in a capacious chromed cage.
The macrocosm was their stage as she flipped a page
 in the chapter of the romantic suspense.
Incense and sweet emanations of chamomile,
lavender and bergamot scent diffused onto the beach and hence,
the damsel with a row of pens wrote poetry and owned a phonograph
 with ballad songs she loved to play.

She pendulated her head from side to side
 all throughout the spring month of May.
Fair Quiet, into the Great Barrier Reef of colourful coral polyps
 and a land of aqua streams
Into the darkness of the twilight with fresh flowers
 gripped in her fingertips under the moonlight beams.

Her partners await'd her on the sea bed she explor'd,
Cardinals, Angels and Lepidochelys olivacea swum circling her underwater
More terrified than anything she gasp'd for air in the depth of the caliginosity
The mantle rays as her villains with shivery limbs as the sea deemed her as its daughter.

She shrilled aloud to the voltage of the lightning bolts
Terawatts forming luminous waves between cumulonimbus clouds and the ground
Fires burnt heavily on the oceanfront as planetary winds blew Archontophoenix alexandrae around
Nearer and nearer she reach'd the shore, floating like a manatee, body sandy
Drops down suddenly like a tired grampus, vertigo craving W ispa Gold candy.

THE ARTISTIC ECLECTIC

They bewildered the fashion admirers in Liechtenstein with their style.
It was ye, COCO Electrika and thou punctilious poodle that held hands for a while.
The center of attention was in their Greek marble stepping stone.
She promenaded down the ramp with the impetus of a water gun.
Her savoir-f aire oozed f ashion as she enthralled everyone.
Speed slackens now as the sultry music starts and before a crowd that is full of bliss,
her walk gets swifter and yet quicker as the tune changes when the lights begin to show.

Electrika's garment was layered with roses, tiger lilies and hibiscuses.
This illustrated her as an exotic aristocrat with an eclectic dernier cri of can-can.
The ornaments were inklike and white which was not conventional.
Watch the wind blow in her hair and the rainbow as her tent with her hand on her heart,
And soonest the best Palomino horses with their chestnut coats walk'd alongside her with allure and 'haute'.

The couturier did not distress as his toggery was ubiquitous.
And our very hopes came to life,
W ith the presentation of the king cheetah with a Schiavona sword and a shield
Much pleasure to its strong nerves and its breathing soft and low
into the eyes of Coco Electrika the fashion bee.
Her inner cheetah character snarl'd at the audience before her,
And in an atmosphere of eeriness and suspense the music altered
again.
Her body locomoted to the vintage tune
 while she flickered a giant golden feather.

THE GRUDGE

O waste of decenniums and starry nights of romance!
Animus and dysphoria underestimate their hurt.
'Twas her lover''s youth that hath been the perfidy
 And the amaurotic eye that cremated the love.
The portals are opening and stairways creak with the likes of each other''s infidelity!

Brutus was her reflection, the contriving beast!
Toiled hands and notoriety hath written seismic lines over his face.
Disgrace! Her nails scrape stripes of acrimony across walls of
time. Introspection of murder and grief threaten''d his existence.
The paradisiacal heavens forbid her impulsions and chains restrict their animosity!

W hat is this moment of lull with thieves in his sheets?
A midnight robber. A devastated lover.
A shattered armor. Another disingenuous face.
A body of f eculent plagues. A mysterious wig.
W hat is affluence and regalia without loyalty?
An octavio of mockery. An aisle of mistrust and disgust.
A forbidden road. Regret.

The ground shakes under their feet as the magnitude did in S haanxi, Kansu and
China. Bholo, Katrina and Hugo were witnesses to her testimony in court.
A haughty look as Tutankhamun and a stream of lies lay on his heavy tongue
as the coquette creature of dalliance had been bought.
She sat on a jellyfish stool with hauteur like a dozen peacocks from SriLanka.
Her eyes had been on his net worth of millions in the Milanese Banca.

To stand and withstand was her new motto as she gaz'd at the Alps surrounding the
Mediterranean in a Slovenian grotto.
Her ideal husband was the portrait of Michelangelo Merisi da Caravaggio.
He'd paint her a picture like Lisa Del Giocondo and build a palace in memory of her like Mumtaz Mahal.
But these matters are superficial and perhaps make people feel special.
Sometimes flowers are the best friends to have as they personif y beauty
and loyalty as a divorcee's sum is settled.

A row of flames lit the way to a woman that loathes death,
Gasping f or her very last breath, diving out of a
Technoavia,
Gliding in the air like a Limosa lapponica
W ithout fear, retracing the spiritual grazes from a man of many faces
Some don't favor virtue and he gave his gifts to his mistress pet
W hom from a thousand daggers came, into bed she wed his vows

And she say'st at evenings when he f orsaketh
her, W hile resting in bed alone f or the sake of this
pity
Sad experiences awake at the gloom of midnight
Stretched f orth longing arms towards bedroom windows after a fight
Feeding rancor gritting hatred''s teeth calling on an ancestry of blight .

There he courted this siren who felt appassionato with currency
Twins in her womb as leverage and what a pair they made
Never-ending opprobrium as earth exhaled its judgment on a woman laid
Bygone days in secret chambers, Russkaya ruletkas and intimate wagers

Landing f eet on the ground throwing a love pendant onto dirt
The clouds and her parted ways as she was kept captive in their cushions
Discovering new spheres in lif e holding revenge over where she was
hurt Lonesome in a summit of revenge, pledging never to be attached
again In this deep turmoil and so distant was its vertex, haunting her
memory.

He feared he'd see her again before they lay him in the tomb;
Acerbity from the past, quondam lover with the horrible humbug.
O if he awoke every day unhappy with expectations of doom
Lugubriousness entertained her while laying on his Persian rug,
His languishing should he not allow to humor her for his emotional death sooths her.

Somnolent in a nursery of Queen Anne's lace and foxgloves
Magnetized by their purity, bosom buddies showcasing love
Under adumbral pine trees grieving over wasted youth
Rancorous from the sour odours of life knowing the truth
Never again will she wed or lay herself with another in bed.

MR PENURIOUS

Smitten by scintillas of common wheat.
Soiled f eet. His grimace paints an icon of tribulation.
W hat is a day without a humble collation?

No fealty and hours of chicanery.
A smirk with no teeth.
A lacuna in space.
A desecrated race. Land of sand and without a serene oasis in sight.

Clouds descend into the desert, weighing their capacity bursting blood
„Tis a city of rondavels and a secret society.
Tears of injustice wail for years in the percipience of its citizens.
W hat is crystallized honey with a bag of rice and no money?

Weeping progenitors agonizing over their descendants in the back of beyond
The weak curse the sky pledging their malevolence to the weather's savage sound.
He cogitates about the lifeless bodies of his neighbors burning under the August sun.
Bruis'd from noontide's flogging rays weeping undraped while holding his head
down.

A Bactrian camel with a limp tongue and anhydrous weather forecasts a future of struggle.
His clavicles jot signs of hunger and sliced rags cover his head.
A Cerastes vipera in the distance hisses with force over its territory.
A fighting spear in its eye and a battle axe in its throat kept the venom
away. Death and starvation are on the f aces of the children.

W here does his pain take him?
As if the earth would not whistle a drop of rain for a feeble man who is almost insane.
Schizophrenia and tortur'd by a shore of wind-swept sand along with the footprints of the
Lamb.
One pathway leads from here and never in his lif e of madman strif e,
did he see a golden c oin consider'd to be the lucky token dazzling in this
road. Years felt like centuries without faith.
W hat is a penurious man's lif e without good health, any wealth and a wife?

W hy can't the planet stand in silence to address his demands?
And with tears flowing along with his shuddering f ears, hopes for new plans
Hast thou no remorse for a yammering f ellow from Cairo,
W hose heartbeat cripples pointing to the north desiring a Turkish gyro?

No comfort in motionless air which chok'd his last breaths
Uneasy from despondency ready to shut down meeting the grave
In this realm of ashes breaking the traipse with his soul being wrenched
Can find no reason to battle being devotional to mortality
From ev'ry depth of his being with veins as roots, lay him in an underground cave.

CHERUB ON A CIRROCUMULUS

'O little planet, thou art busy like a pollen bee", said thee.
The grandiose seven seas are filled with astonishing subaqueous palaces.
The continents and archipelagos are enshrouded with native flora and fauna.
W hy does life seem so feckless to some of the cosmos's society?

They misuse each day to junctures of rueing and bemoaning.
The purpose of each period is a new enigma to one's lif e.
Take not for grant'd the heirlooms and gifts one has while he is alive.
Bear with each other, she'd say to persons of foreign tongues
W hilst unwinding on the cirrocumulus staring down at those with tobacco bongs.

Flurries of ice and powder snow settle onto the ground.
The thunder roars and monsoons patrol the metropolis of lights.
The populace hullabaloo that their exorbitant paraphernalia are tarnished and
buried. The turbulent wind is a hound.
Its sound tramples as the Sokolnicheskaya Line in the Moscow metro,
And an equestrian thoroughbred stampede bordering around.

W here do cataclysms originate and why was this our fate?
The cherub spies on the occupants below in sudden curiousity.
She gingerly strokes her invaluable harp rendering music for the age of hypocrisy.
In the twinkle of one's eye they are retrospecting over what is lost.
O what cost!
The land is obliterated and there is no escape.
Diminutive door that she knocks as a harbinger of hope f or their sake.

RAINBOW EMPRESS: A STORY OF HIGH FASHION

O bittersweet, blizzard blue and jazzberry
jam.
Colours that glittereth on the gown in the Classical Cepheid
The woman's flourescent toes sunk into the pacific blue ocean while soaking in the sun.
The sea green palms shadowed her behind as the wind blew glittery starlets that sparkled
everywhere.

Her name Majesty was written with red-knobbed starfish in the tumbleweed shore.
The tropical rainforest was her empire and in it held a golden door.
The secret was the key and its code was timberwolf.
Tickle me pink belladonna lilies surround'd her on the polygon floor.
Majesty smiled at her reflection in the diamond mirror at the illusion that Dame Nature had created.

Razzle dazzle rose and Robin's egg blue were the streaks in her power blown
hair.
The fashion empress opened the show with a grand entrance that was one fit for outer space.
The shamrock vines were her accessories while the mystic pearl sunset became the backdrop of her
gown.
Pixie powder and princess perfume sparkled on her skin as her jasmine scent revivified the Milky W ay.
She jumped on a lemon glacier felucca and sightsaw another terra firma.

The Caribbean currents pulled her in against the steel blue
waves.
Periwinkle and pink flamingo were the bands that welcomed her to this new
haven.
There stood sonic silver.
Its illuminating emeralds glistened in the cyber grape sky.
The fashion was in her irridescent colour and glitz was her lips.
The rainbow empress danced to the melodies of the red salsa rays that scorched her light years away.
Cotton candy and bubble gum marshmallows were her audience endorsing her sensation, mode and
allure.

THE SWAN ROMANCE

W hat are two creatures with napes alike?
They are both bedazzled by each other's sight.
Their f ascination comes with their dulcif ying grace,
as their faces rub benevolently against each other bef ore the hominine race.
W elcoming the assemblage with W olfgang's symphony from Prague
In our adulthood days ringing merry bells while meadowlarks sang.

The lakelets of Lucerne swirl gelatinous whirlpools forming a floor for their whirl.
Lilies are their concomitants, waterfalls are their sinfoniettas and the mountaintops are their devotees.
Their bodies drift away as the white swan gives an acute glance.
His reticent nature and sleek inclination adds to his captivation.

Crown'd with quality and scents of Madagascar Vanilla diffused into the troposphere
Every rocky Alpine height hiding colour spectrums and celebration from Newton
Rapscallions shadowing the canton inspecting as bloodhounds in sudden fear.
Moral virgins taking notes at the spectacle competing in invidiousness there.

The charcoal swan's symmetry and equanimity is enjoy'd by her loyal partner.
Their ardency and adoration encompasses their purview in the sparkling
water. They wear coronals of orchids as the sun glistens on their innocence.
Dear Cygnus, what's a romance without two swans in love as Streptopelia risorias?

The chemistry hoisted their imponderous wings to fly in the fresh oceanic sky.
The crowds were ecstasized by their comportment and smiles brought a new light.
O windy hamlet populated by faces of mesmerized lovers!
They stare in marvel at the sincerity of these feathered wonders.
The sunset came and the cascades moderated under the moonlight.
A solacing melisma came from the Stradivarius while the swan romance was finalized f or the
night. Pyrotechnics blazed as the sweetlings smooched their adieus of affection in the province of
twilight.

Victory and wedded bliss, a lovely kiss with Versailles Charm and Poetic Muse
Honeymoon in Kapellbrücke laying on light Victorian rose silks in a cot
Nestling briefly to join in a dance of Danish Bournoville ballet relevé-ing as Pavlova
Similar to a canvas from Edgar Degas twin to seraphs while the pair entertained each other.

Intimacy and courtly love educated with time
Cease not this affair that start'd off as a perf ect
rhyme Relations without struggles fertilizing under
torches Faint at the view, drown'd in tears at the
ritual.

PEACOCK PARADISE

Pheasant bird of ostentatious magnetism, both bold and piercing.
Her vivid violet garb blanketed her squinny physique with round crimson cheeks.
She wore her dress with swish and sass in the ritzy intelligentsia.
Poui perennials lay on the ground bef ore her proud crowd.

The peacock's parade in Punjab was steady, silentious and flirtatious in the expo.
The stratosphere poured diamonds and golden glitter unto her that shimmered bubbles of beauty.
Fuschia hibiscuses poised observing her while oscillating to the acapellas of the opera toucans.
The bird squeezed a basket of strawberries and blueberries that she threw artistically at her visitors.

A guest overture came with an ivory white peacock whose plumage simulated akoya pearls from the Pinctada Fucata
Chemnitzii. O what convivality on such an effulgent evening!
The royal blue balneal coruscated with aqua ripples as the peacock strolled over the wistaria wooden bridge.
Greetings to the coterie who digest lily bedizened c hocotejas from the natural fridge.
W hy, these two species comparable with egos that fight!
Do birds of a feather truly flock together?

Courtyards of swaggerers confederating at an Indochinese Tiffin
Pavo Muticus on the royal throne in Burma sitting
Posing as a statuette while an illustrator sketch'd her demeanor
Carried on a chariot before the province of peacocks wearing Chinchilla fur

Pairidaeza, pairidaeza how euphonious art thou;
Timeless, peace and prosperity for a city of festive peacocks that bow
Rondo Alla turca on a dozen nadaswarams and Shehnais in a world of adventurous imagery,
Arise from their cloaks flashing their proportions, amour-propre mixed with abstract artistry.

Academicians and savants composing theorems of a peacock's mental health
Recalcitrant to adjustment dismissing humility due to physical wealth
For mundane things ne'er transf orm and so atop a church's steeple one may stand
Haughty as can be stamping beaver tale tiles swearing her supremacy o'er the land.

LA MIA STELLA BRILLANTE

O luminescing star from Andromeda, thou art scintillant and
conflagrant! Ye simulacrum is a world unspoken and savvied only by an
outlander. Thou years are vernal and confidential with the night sky.
Thou fingers sweat fireflies that concoct streams of Darya-ye Noor and gems.
Life's meaning is trivialized without your Sirius starlight and presence.

Thou art burning universal riches and thou scent is more redolent than gardens of jasmine.
O far thou art and bef ore me is your perspicacity.
Thou shooting star is a sprinter and it already won its chase.
If only the phalanges of our cosmos could touch and kiss each other's lips.
It is an imaginable beauty to attest thou gift and f ormula.
La Mia Stella Brillante thou art a magnum opus in the lake of Arcturus dreams.

Please unshackle me from all otiose memories of the past.
My heart waits long hours in this mood of misery.
I hanker thou tender touch and spiritual clutch that I have craved so much.
Our ecumenical worlds are contiguous but yet so distant.
For how the spacecraft ye embarked on felt like ages and Lilium Longiflorums ago.

My heart must be liberated f or this feeling is
supernatural. W hy did ye forsake me for another
treasure?
Thou f ace lays in the heart of my Peridot pendant.
Perpetually shall these initials rest in my piece.
This message is f aith and that is all I accredit.
Through the toilsome times and pugnacious weather my heart shall endure.
Forever is our posture and we sitteth its height.

Non posso vivere senza voi
Gradisco voi di più e più
Sempre il mio cuore è per voi
Said I to my one true love magnifying my speech
Slumbering on my sand pillow in Maldives on the beach

Times would pass as an imaginative traveller,
Cooking oriental sweetlips, lobsters and
snappers
Having visions under the nimbus of Boracay and perhaps someday,
I'd return to Plage de la Bouillabaisse and eat gastronomic cuisine
Laying eyes on my star hoping it would return to dine with me.

Lubov'-eto to, shto nel'z'a pon'at holovoy,
yeye nuzhno pochuvstvovat' sercem.
Embracing a postcard that a Bubo virginianus brought to my den
Вот моё сердце. Оно полно любви.
Vot moe serce. Ono polno lubvi.

Teardrops from the constellation and luminosity beyond f antasy
Picking petals from Leontopodium alpinum delivered from Romanian Carpathians
'Il m'aime, il ne m'aime pas', declared I reminiscing lovingly
How youthful are the lineaments of a star and a suite as large as the Parthenon
W ith pleasant tidings inviting my existence to the Notre Dame de Paris

Agendums of sacrament, a destiny without blight
Safe with arrival and a relationship without spite
A woman chained by her memories never letting go
Chirping politely to the starry galactic halo in the spiral sky

Fue flechazo on a catamaran in Le Meridien Bora Bora
Floating away from an island of dense tropical flora.
Tu eres mi luz en la oscuridad y mi alma gemela
There he rested in the sapphire interstellar space
Con af ecto, I sang descant while the waves crash'd playing bass

Alle Dingen eerlijk, there is love even when flesh is weak
Du sopade av mig mina f ötter
Och jag har bara ögon f ör dig
I would've climbed as far took me to Mount Otemanu at the highest peak

O fervid lover, meditating in a Hypnos bed
Susurrating utterances of when we'd finally wed
Or perhaps to reach closer to you, I'd take a trip to Kenya
on a hot air balloon ride at midnight, above the Masai Mara.

Drowsy motions o'er a point on the celestial bridge Steps closer
to my sweet above the Mid-Atlantic ridge Hardingfeles echoing
with skill, outsretched arms to my God's will
W alking on cloud tops, disremembering my sorrows and with this Holy Spirit I" m filled.

THE PELICAN FIGHT

A doublet of pelicans had a plan to eat a piquant fish.
They came from different territories off the littoral of little Tobago.
A behemothic pelican entitled Abbott and a peewee pelican
named Bruno wanted this golden fish as their dish.
Abbott was stalwart with a massive mouth and he was smart.
He took one stare at the golden fish and wanted to rip it apart.

His only obstacle was Bruno but he saw him as small.
That made him better in his perception as he made a bird call.
His eyes were glued to the prey's slothful movements in the sea.
Abbott moved from left to right in the firmament and aimed his head with glee.
Suddenly, Bruno snagged the glittering fish out of the water and gobbled it in a gulp.
He cachinnated at Abbott and eructed in his face.
Abbott was in a state of consternation at Bruno's behaviour
who did not divvy and give him a taste.

Abbott decided to initiate a fray because he was hurt.
Bruno flew away returning to the coast he came from.
Abbott dashed behind him with plans of making him his meal.
Eventually, he caught up with Bruno and it was a done deal.

The pelicans commenced tussling as Bruno justified himself.
He flew into a grotto and Abbott followed in after with a bolt.
They both collided into a giant stone and were in another zone.
It was very crepuscular as there was no light.
These two pelicans regretted starting the fight.
Abbott yearned to leave the place as he could not watch Bruno in his face.
It was disturbing to him that he was both voracious and
blind. He deemed the actions of Bruno as very unkind.

THE DOLPHIN SYMPHONY

In a big lagoon, lived a silver bottlenose dolphin.
She serenaded every daybreak as she digest'd shellfish as a snack.
The coral reefs were her associates and they all form'd a pack.
The seaweeds came together and they were cerise, mahogany and green.
They played bepop with the oysters while the dolphin swam into the scene.

She sang high pitch and low pitch, twirling in a circle.
The lagoon was her resting ground and in came a loggerhead turtle.
The turtle luxuriated in hearing her sing.
Her pirouetting got f aster and the bubbles formed a ring.
The Caribbean Sea alone with the western waves rippled down the leeward chain.
W here all the dolphins splashed in the limitless deep were swordfish competing in their sleep.

A fleet of Costa Rican dolphins came to visit the lagoon.
They came to sing a symphony under the radiating moon.
The stars were the witnesses as they looked down in the sea.
The bottlenose dolphin pac k turned into an underwater party.
Dolphins tail slapping to the left.
Dolphins spy hopping to the right.
A symphony of Delphinidae and tropical birds gazing
into the bubbly ocean of white.

THE BUTTERFLY LESSON

The empire of the emperor butterfly stood tall above the town.
This town was occupied by a clown who often did frown.
Mr. Clown had a face of red, black and white.
He was the national star and his wings were the shape of a kite.
The emperor often made jokes of everything as he sat on his throne.
In a giant garden he lived but in his heart he was all alone.

One day a new visitor had arrived in his kingdom.
She brought tropical friends of colours both bold and bland.
The emperor butterfly thought she was the most marvelous in the land.
The clown brought his new queen to live in a buttercup.
They sat and drank tea of nectar with cream petals.
His queen had a name. Her name was Fame.
Fame wished to take the place of the emperor as the ruler.
She wanted his crown jewels and the treasure garden.
The garden was filled with thousands of flowers and trees.
The birds chirped songs up and down alongside the bees.

Fame sat on the sovereign's chair in the lily chamber.
The clown smiled and told her she could stay.
She was astounded but as he was a clown, he wanted to laugh.
The czar had a plan to break her wings.
This portended that she could not fly.
He wished to see her seated and most likely die.
Fame was exultant to be seated wearing the emperor's crown.
But the emperor soon unleashed his plan to also see her
frown.

He summoned the rain as he spoke to Mother Nature.
She cradled her butterfly child as she loved the garden they lived in.
The deluge fell and it broke the wings of Fame.
This brought her shame.
The harlequin smiled again, clutching his crown.
He told her that she should have stayed his queen.
Fame snivelled bitterly that she could no longer fly while laying on the
loam. The summery palace that she once lived in was no longer her home.

THE FUNKY URBANITE

Sophistication convergeth with fashion.
A fantasy f oretold.
She was ultra retro, a meritorious starlet and one that hath never engaged in a fight.
W ith what point to prove?
Her enemies were taken care of as she pranced with a groove.
She snapped her fingers with a pout as her height was a sight.

Her edginess showed with a towering, tawny fohawk with white streaks.
For how the Funky Urbanite's hair was straight, sleek and as long as two feet.
Her f ashion ensemble was a testimonial all by itself.
Deck'd with heliotrope Leopardus pardalis print skin that was snug against her bones,
She wore knee high sandals like a gladiator in Roma
And in her hand stood a Strawberry gelato cone.

The steps she tapped, the hands that clapped
The audience lauded moderately and she was vain
Falling into a trance piercing the ground with arrows like archery
There's character in her prance as the fashion took over her brain
On went she, methinks that the show could not have been better

Funky Boondocks was the peninsula motherland she was born in.
She rode an Icon Sheene and it expedited to the sound of the efficacious
engine. There-her rings symbolized her name and she flashed them to the
crowd.
She smacked her lips administering crimson gloss and swung her arms across.

Mademoiselle's booties strolled the runway ramps and one held an astro lamp.
It illuminated with every footf all she made and following this, the fashion model got paid.
Is the time of a funky urbanite mocking the minor feat that she once had adorning her figure with Jóias and
gems? The lightning in her eye strikes,
 And a grin like the chessy cat widens while conversing with her clique of friends.

THE PROMISE

Cherished memories in Groot-Zundert,
For how they were authentic and true.
Nothing dismayed them.
Their seeds have already sown,
And so they never wasted any time.

Yesteryear played a treasured melody
And you were no exception to it.
However, it was destiny f or us to part ways.
Beginners all commence somewhere.
You've smiled on me old recollection so too shall I smile on you.

Those who did not welcome my companionship with open arms,
how f ate speaks differently f or them as a bolt from the blue.
W hy give up the certitude when time has turned its back on you.
Let the Nimbostrati and Cumulonimbi bring droplets of drizzle down.
Trivialize your adversaries from Gehenna for their ears hear the thunder sound.

Memories speak words unspoken,
so don't speak anything f or them.
Speaking does nothing for the speaker but speaking.
For destiny welcomes you with its red carpet,
as you alone walk on it.

No time to reminisce, love pursueth not itself to please.
But heavenly powers upon a woman whose heart needs
ease. A place of rest and sleep, f or as long as eternity.
Life in a lonely world with shadows and spirits battling against thy soul
W ith fiends and angels at opposite ends, taking naked bodies to the grave that cannot mend
Good immortal souls above the exospheres, and evil tarnished souls to torture beneath the inner core

Comparable to a scene from Ludovico Carracci,
The angels Seraphim, Michael, Ariel and Raphael all ascended into dreamland holding hands
To this promise one questions merrily:
W here and how do we go holding our palms on our hearts to these perpetual cherubic
lands? All in ivory attire, standing bef ore the alpha tree with two scrolls of lif e and death.
There stood a celestial light with the moon behind and diamonded the path to the promised highway's bet.

An Amerigo Vespucci appeared in the vault of heaven
Jumping on this vessel there stood saints in a line of
seven Esteeming poised beauty after a life of missions
performed
Cheering on with approval letters on streets of gold in a place airborne.

In the flash of a megalight year, behind Galactic spheroids
Beyond imagination, in a transcendental realm and no meteoroids
Deserves the surname 'everlasting' after a lif e of self-sacrificing
In fear of a divine being without the curse of an apple and no fighting.

THE GLOVE

O glove, where did doth go?
It was the eventide of Venezia's summer ball.
Thou atramentous lace captivated me as ye fed my fashion.
My arm jived with thou touch as we f ell deeply in love.

The phosphorescence, cameras and action were our
corroborators. O for how they were impassioned.
Old kodachromes hold our memory distant.
W here have ye absconded to old crony? The answer is lost.
The electa pocket chronograph striked midnight as we were preordain'd to settle down.

W atch our f or one's owner as she wishes ye well.
Her orisons echo every nightfall f or thou emergence.
And into Piazza San Marco I ran looking for my beloved one and there the shadow of her lace lay,
Seated in the basilica beneath the splendid Ascension dome but only time will tell.
And on this day, glove do come back to my hand,
for I had travelled long hours to this misty foreign land.

W hat is this passion I once had as my bosom beats and my blood boils in the Veneto heat.
And to the top of Tre Cime di Lavaredo I'd climb for my dear glove in the name of love.
Yet I see a strapping lad on a moored gondola in acqua alta from the Giudecca canal with promises of our meet.
By word of mouth, my little glove has gone to rest in San Giorgio Maggiore on a Vividus bed and wi th all that
said, Off we go to capture him and into the deepest night my dark friend I come to rescue while I sigh and cry.

W inding down my worries as I stood perplexed as the gondolier rowed me to the site
Like a painting of Marieschi, the water overflowed and the rumbling, tumbling thunder roared at the arrival of my f antastic
sight. Bolts of lightning flashed in the gloom of the night and the howls of the wind were long and loud
Upon the shore I jumped to search for my precious glove where the early morning waves rippled
'Tis the time to celebrate as the glove was about to meet her mistress while my love
tripled, And the stars of the night lended their light to I on the Insula Memmia.

The fair breeze blew as the moonlit door of the Teatro Verde opened with my glove on the bed
I bear witness to my dear friend as I grabbed her bef ore the world, placing her on my arm again
To every one upon this terrestrial sphere and during the Eine Nacht in Venedig operetta,
I raised my arm with this lace glove in all silvery white and without a doubt, she could not do better.

The beauty of the morning came with the horizon sunrise as my brawny consort and I escaped
together on this quiet day we sped on the cigarette boat against the hungry tides in the sunny weather.
And miles away to Milan we head,
we meet the terra firma to change our ensemble and in fashion sense,
I unleashed my gown of peacock feathers like a bridal dress
W ith purple polyantha roses in my hand with one black glove on, let no man mock our
vogue. And light laughter holding our mood, willingly we walk with a prance, style and a
groove.

Life's a pleasant romance f or my esteemed glove and I,
strolling bef ore the Duomo di Milano so deeply in love as I stared into the sky
Sweet day, full of surprises in this land with my loyal accomplice, walking on
Like a view from Polaris, the earth rotates towards the east and we feast as we got married
Our pledge to never part again, dare I hold my peace to my weariness, the pyrexia and the devoir I carried.

Oh Italy! Tis the time to depart, and the gentleness of the evening breeze
Caress'd my emotions disappearing in a whirlwind of silent powder
Motions over the ocean flying to Principat de Mónegue with God's help
Gliding to the Opéra de Monte-Carlo f alling on my knees

Hearing an introduction et Rondo Capriccioso and the Carnival of the animals
Into a deep sleep I fall with my glove,
to awake in a room of Champagne Noir Soy candles
W iping one's eyes into a 'Mir iskusstva', with prima ballerinas pirouetting

O Impressionism and composition,
W ithin a Degas painting in the Fogg museum
Melodizing with the glove in the air
Nor loud, nor soft.
A filling tune in the atmosphere.

And in the middle of the night, came a Chordeiles minor neotropicalis
Turning my back to the site and on to Saint Petersburg
This merry tale I tell while sitting in the Marinsky Theatre
Above all in the Tsar's Box listening to the Queen of Spades, writing a letter

Risen from my seat with the power of a prima ballerina assoluta
To dance on stage with my glove to the Swan Lake waltz
As Preobrazhenskaya and Kschessinskaya did without any f alls
Releasing my jitters and letting lose my feet, enjoying the beat.

Suddenly I ran out of the opera and onto a Cygnus olor's back
A few strong birds accompanied us to our last destiny
W here every fascination lasted in Port-of-Spain in a city so dark
Raqs baladi from the Victorian era below a sky of firework sparks
Shimmies with the glove, staccatos and undulations
W hat is my life without my love through trials and tribulations?

RUTHLESS WORLD

The glories of human flesh, the weakness es of the skin, dwelling in a world of slavery sin
Most care about f ollowing the unethical norm and need f ortitude to do what is considered right
Gang fights, murderers, terrorists, pain and sorrow at its height
Condemning fingers, judgmental eyes, unf orgiveness and jealous kin
Men being led by women like Adam and Eve in Eden did,
The stronger we grow, more hatred they f eel and power strikes them like an electric eel

The wretched conceit of cruel men who hold race, religion and gender dear to their hearts
And as fast as supersonic speeds that crack motion here on earth, some never find their rebirth
Over the highest peak of Chomolungma and lowest land of the Dead Sea, the world won't change f or anybody
Class separation from a Marxist's view and a curious man sitting on a pauper's stone scorning inequality and the
bourgeoisie's financial worth. Rifles, deringers, Jerichos and chaucats shooting men like in their Führer und Reichskanzler
Hitler's reign
And suicides like Eva Braun"s after accompanying him in their quests of human pain.

Dead Sea scrolls of papyrus tell the history of God's people that science greatly condemns
W atch the dust from the slow hot wind blow in the deserts of Northern Africa and Colorado
And hear the chiming of Big Ben go while the beating rain stimulates the whips on slaves in early Trinidad and Tobago
Ruthless world.
„Tis a heartless world. No mercy for Yeshua bef ore Pontius Pilate in „Ecce Homo" as he died between two penitent thieves
How the world reeks of injustice and crime in ages of many who have been deceived.

Various mentalities based on socialization and one grand continent of Pangaea,
And from the beginning of time, the citizens of the cosmos slept in a global city of danger
Our times are articles in future files, people battling against the presence of stalkers and pedophiles
Council of Clermont plotting to retrieve religious lands and Columbus bringing slavery to the islands
Deaths of the Tainos in slave markets in Seville, and crashing of world trade towers that took years to build
Innocent lives shunned by anaconda eyes, mocking family and serenity in the W estern world

W heezing men running for their lives,
From speeding clouds grabbing flesh, as were Mount T ambora's pyroclastic flows
Conflagrant sea of flames reducing men to ashes, f alling out of windows head first in the ruthless world
Creations degraded by the Ku-Klux Klan dressed in white with burning crosses in Mississippi
Harmless Negroes afflicted mentally and physical harm in treacherous times over nef arious vainglory.
Self-murders in destructive territories with explosives and grenades, demolishing structures similar to a flurry.

One saw the horrid looks of a stolen abandoned child and there was the wolf in sheep's clothing
cry Criminals leading the youth's wild minds along with those just looking for an excuse to be
unkind Hypocrites and critics with evil mouths that don't fix themselves but are willing to put others
down The nightmare of a hollow society with human devils lower than hell's breathing ground
Playing games with no care as far as their guns go with whispers and tender looks into their victim's eye

Looking fixedly at a Mechanized Celestial Globe in one's hands
Spinning from west to east analyzing the continents and its many lands,
Smooth beginnings to rough ends, methought that the world was a capsule
A tale in an endless time, one mocks the wrath of ruthless men
Of solid f aith for six thousand years mentally roaring in the lion's den

But there's quiet humility that bans the pessimism away,
And only can a true optimist say, while sitting on the branches of a Buttonball tree,
Staring at fire and carpenter ants working hard to build empires in the forest's leaf y sea
Not to dwell in the past with hopes for a better lif e in a peaceful world and ne"er to stray.

THE ROSE

I saw a great showy rose in a Victorian conservatory preserved from winter's harsh winds
And Inside the glass shone a golden love letter stating several things,
To my cherished rose, you ought to know in this note of prose
Pack your suitcases and leave in the middle of the night
Take the midnight train to London and into the West Indies on a flight

The rose in all of its splendour with water droplets on her petals
A plane of passengers gathering together drinking hot rose tea from ceramic kettles
I am aware of her age and now the weather has changed in Caribbean territory
A plan to return her into a lovely Rosaceae garden with her family to live became mandatory

Let lif e shine on her innocent beauty and elegance as long as this season lasts
I met a large garden of Rosa Carolinas, Rosa muscosas, albas and damasks
Holding her gently I layed her on the grass, inhaling the oxygen gas
Then I felt like running into a field in Montego Bay near a natural pond
Softly I touch a hybrid tea rose with virtuousness, fragrance and kneeling on the ground,
I bestow my osculations upon the Aureolin flower and the elements brought a light shower.

Up some stairs into a nebulous aviary surrounded with Rosa pimpinellifolia
Groups of Rosa Oxyacantha and my nursemaid" s daughter gathering her paraphernalia
Budgerigars, Blue Mountain Lorikeets and cocktails dining together with Synstylae
In love with Picasso's rose period and to account for Cézanne as a Femme au Chapeau.

I am covered with Aeolic wrodons sprinkling rose oil in the air
Hesperiidae, Papilionidae, Nymphalidae fluttering everywhere
Twirling round and round in my Shangri-la with arms wide open
Hundreds of pleased playmates but only one that caught my
eye
In the moment I skip with a sprightly yawn while the cumuli all sigh

Mój kwiatuszku.
May we rest together as the Do-khyi plays the Japanese Shakuhachi,
Hearts beating, cheeks meeting and away we go laying on the lawn
Hugging a triplet of Champagnes d'Argent snuggling after being
born Nuzzling under le Chêne à Papineau, hugging Dakimakuras

O rose thy reverence, purity and secrecy
How one admires thee.
Thy beauty, colour and versatility.
Long live your modesty in this dwelling place with new beginnings.

In my lap rests a Rosa gymnocarpa as an infant child
Innocent as can be, elusive rose as Moses in the river Nile;
Matter of a mysterious form, veiled with coral petals
Greater to me it is than precious metals.

CHRONICLES OF CANICHE

Living her span on a royal pillow in Neuschwanstein Castle
She glances outside her bedroom window at a f amily of Hirundinidae,
The snowy Alps and a panorama of the Schwansee below her painting from Claude Monet.
For some reason the obedient princess kept her black eyes on these migrant birds,
Analyzing their freedom to fly in the illimitable sky leaving her lost for words.

She is bitter and lonesome as her main friend is her mistress
And fluffy cushions such as Jupiter, Pluto, Saturn and Uranus,
Lended their ear to her melancholy barks while a servant clipped her nails
Her name is Principessa and in her f ortress, her curly fur blows while reading her fan mail

Some call her Frizzerella and others call her Tinkerella with her pampered pride
One day she received a great package that she wore in her carriage outside
A Bargazine Russian Sable while visiting the stables for a ride
Zweibrücken awaiting for a championship show jumping run
Ascending oxers, walls and colorful obstacles as a caniche's way of fun

Mangosteen, Kumquat and Durian, the fairest fruits in the land
Accompanied Principessa to ride into Schwarzwald, searching for a best friend
May'st she finally find one whom she can share her secrets with holding hands
A dutiful sidekick to keep her company while on the train to Poland.

Pulsations travelling on the Maglev to meet one's opponent
Onward to Zamek wawelski to fight the shadow of Smok W awelski
Into the Renaissance courtyard they go, Zweihänders clanging
And like the gladiators in the Roman republic, entertain'd were the public

Continuing her quest, into the Smocza Jama the shadow ran
Returning back to the castle on a Friesian horse, Tinkerella
sang Falling bef ore Jupiter, Mercury and Virtue,
In love with Giovanni di Niccolò de Luteri.

Sitting in the Kurza Stopka, pondering of sailing the seas
For she travelled to a land so f ar and holding many keys
She chose the Lamborghini Reventon, driving into the streets of Poland
Headed to the Morze Bałtyckie, with many on Frizzerella's mind.

Looking to the sky, singing an aria for a fidus Achates
Twas many days that went by, waiting for this friend
Perhaps he'd emerge out of the sea, while sipping some honey tea.
W aterfalls from the wild blue yonder as the caniche wonder'd

W alking toward the shore, stood a group of Laridae
A Larus argentatus stared at her, vying for the title
Oh but anything and anyone could be her confidant
Once one was lively, a steadf ast ally and confident.

To dwell forever and to lightly dance their first foxtrot
Under the stars, charmed f or the night holding its rights
Into a vintage cage resting on the rocks
Geometry of a solar eclipse holding its face giving him a kiss

W onderment under the umbras, penumbras and antumbras
in a faraway land she traversed, headed to Rome in December
Visions of Fontana di Trevi for a banquet with Agrippa
Mind illusions, ghostly apparitions but inhibitions

Impossible was it for Principessa to reappear at the castle
A common bird such as seagull would bring their schloss shame
Of shape and size too diddly from the hoi polloi, untamed.
Upon whose character flew over the Mare Balticum, searching for game.

Silence to their notions, holding him in a carriage
She'd rather live in mökki in Finland with her
baggage But a nightmare it'd be for the titividated
pooch
She wear'st an immaculate coat as the interior of cabbage

They said their adieus while she jotted her diary notes
Shamefaced, aggrieved, released flying away peeved
Of few words she wrote, she hopped into an air boat
Onward to mirth in Ludwig's suite throwing off her coat.

THE LILY IS A MYSTERY

Lily so distinct.
Why are thy petals closed?
What does thou hide inside with such pride?
O nymphaeaceae, in the Musée de l'Orangerie
I question the Brasenia and Ondinea.

Is your window frightened of change?
Does the environment shatter thy trust?
Sophistication says mouthfuls of ingenuity
Water watches her exterior in wonder.
Why is she so different?

Adam's ale waves her a welcome,
Yet her arms stay crossed.
The glasses all tingle,
Dating her inferior.

The moon tells her speech
When seeing the ground.
Aqua pura spells her strength,
But she doesn't give in.
Give the lily a chance.
She'll open eventually.

TRIANGULUM AUSTRALE

Braizier, Libbi and Apolonija
The calamitous love triangle.
W hom did he love more?
He had no respect for women,
He called them all whores.

Bordellos, prophylactics, intergalactic
Stroboscopic light, ecdysiasts and bars
Lagers, wagers, a lif e without dangers
Smoketh his Arturo Fuente Opus,
-Saying his lif e never had any purpose.

The Master of playing cards, while looking at the guards.
King of Hearts holding his trump card,
W hilst he collects his award, next to his sword.
Parabellum-Pistole, meeting eyes with Libbi.

O but when he refrain'd to look, her ego gave in.
Wedded man with peepers living in sin. Be everything
he wished on her for several nights Robbing his wife's
heart of peace, causing many fights.

There, one day she went away to never turn back
Staring at Ara, Normus and Apus in the night sky
Compare'st them to her lif e with her husband,
sighing
There's no such thing as a honest courtesan with a blunt in her hand
Smiling at Apolonija's photograph, she mock'st seducing her companion.

A woman with legs outstretched dancing burlesque
Speak'st words of magnitude, shaking her head giving attitude.
 His ghetto Mc Laren accelerating, swerving corners violently, smoking Maui wowie
Seeking her mate having made plans to meet her clique of
friends. A room of bachelorettes dealing with business on a
stormy night.

Another day at midday they met, plotting against the death of Braizier
Ah! Heartbreaking sight it was to see her spouse's infidelity
To the private jet, two creatures alike, smooching while embracing her brassiere.
W ailing Apolonija in the bushes, sneering at the lies of his
credibility. For jubilant were he in the arms of another, holding this
new lover.

The mysteries that happened inside the plane, as his wife slowly went insane
Displeased with how well she was treated, panting like a bull, heated
Ne'er again would she let him out of her sight, f or in this blight
Dispelling his inamorata, waving at the nose of the airplane with a red flag
Flabbergasted at her mien, he took great umbrage at her kinesics on the runway

Cumbersome his lingua became and dauntless he were
Squalls to the aviator to vamoose, dressing Libbi in fox
fur W hisking into the boscage, crestf allen and ululating
Obdurate was he and in his legitimate right to be dating
Ingredients of a murderer, loading a W alther PPK threatening his life

Thick as an alligator with the haughtiest heart, and a gun in his hand
Against his own head vacillating as a jape, slowly departing the southern land
His bedmate waving to the chaparral blowing kisses o'er the meridian sun
Provoked Apolonija started blasting her rifle as a bedlamite, doing it for fun.
Cries of a cocaine addict, heedlessly shooting at the aluminium aircraft laughing.

W hile in the welkin, the aeroplane soon landed back in an emergency
Fancies the art of open fire with stifling smoke aborting their pregnancy
But whatsoe'er she did, for ceaseless constancy executing her other half
Could by the world's standards her merciless actions be forgiven?
Swarmed with deleterious spirits, tainted thinking and nerve driven.

Her companions with M192 Lightweight Ground Mounts blasting in the air
As Cherokee Indians in a savage state with war paint,
on their faces whooping inciting fear
Chambers all empty when the army brought them to their last wordly sphere
Like Czolgosz, Rosenberg and Zangara, to the electric chair they went
Their flames awaited them as adrenalin pumped in the nightmare,
condemning her husband as being inferno sent.

CANES VENATICI

Fleeing into the woodlands in the Amazon deep
Hounds growling echoing barks disturbing the village's sleep
And splintery were their teeth searching for juveniles meat
Vampire bats flapping with beating wings o'er those escaping
Cor Caroli in the constellation shining brightly to the people gaping

Vanishing beneath the Bertholletia excelsa,
behind the Astrocaryum jauari
But the dwellers are soundless having climbed the trees
 and tears they carry Humans ordering their gun dogs to collect homunculi after
destroying their homes
Shaking the roots of the jungle, pummelling the lilliputians
with Amazonite and Rhodocrosite stones

Swinging from vine to vine like howlers and spider monkeys
To the place of refuge away from the invasion in the dwarf nation Bonnets
falling into the mouths of danger, ascending to a higher station. Egyptian
tanned skin women looking to the night sky for peace and direction. Chasing
the Canum Venaticorum with its outstandingly red appearance
La superba star conducting them by means of its light to a region of clearance.

W as comforting to see- a city of Barasana people
People of the Panthera onca who morphed into a melanistic jaguar.
The canines gnarled at this creature when they suddenly became feeble
It combated with a large leap and the heart of a Barbary lion beating as a Djembe drum.
Drunkyard hunting dogs retreating in a flash to their constellation shocked and struck
dumb.

Forever gone were the two hounds and yet they, so extraterrestrial and powerful
Left f or their destiny without any sign of e'er seeing them again
Jubilant as can be, allies of the Barasana heading to a new dominion of men.
W hose people were just as miniature as the juveniles to mate and multiply.
Many were massacred in the hunt so onto an area of gentlemen with
stunts.

In a gloomy province, fear sank in their thoughts
 and many blood clots they had Horrors in an unknown land,
 uninvited being watched by men holding torches lighted Raised eyebrows by their
visitors whose betrayal came from the inception of time
Sacred to the firmament a white dove descended dropping a palm between them bef ore the mine
A mine with golden treasures below the sunflower galaxy with morning tables to dine

Flambeaus in hand in a large room of shadows
 to discuss the situation of cohabiting
W ithin this kingdom of newcomers impressing the earth dwellers with wings flapping
Ara ararauna species on their shoulders making a getaway
from the rainforest's precipitation
There sit they in a dungeon-like chamber eating roasted Amorphophallus enjoying this
sensation. Hopes of merging with their partners in a state of mysticism avoiding history's
criticism.

W alking along the granitic path,
They visited the leader of their village- Amorphophallus titanum
O'ergrown with moss was her surroundings in the face of malodorous wrath.
Questions of breeding while placing ringlets as gifts around her staff.
And ladybugs clothe her as she sings the advice rollickingly to the personages.

Only under the full moon, Messier 3 present, the flower chants.
Charmingly f erocious with telescope eyes giving consent to their rants.
Says she- to cross the tributary amidst the piranhas, bewaring of the Serrasalminae.
Hop onto water lilies and float taking saf e measures, steering clear of the snakes.
Moving speedingly to their fate to restore their sabotaged town,
Blending with the jungle like Chamaeleonidae.
To collect the passkey- for ever more to stay with her citizens wearing crowns.

Ignorant from their insanity, the sovereign instructed them to danger
Desperation along with qualm conflicted their cerebration o'er the river
An aqueous death orchestrated by the mother flower quivering
Vines tied their f eet as they f elt def eat laying in a piranha's manger.
W hat power is in their shrieks and childish catastrophe,
In the name of intercourse where all things end meeting death.

THE IMMACULATE HACKER

Hurt by Weltschmerz was this dear butterfly through the operations of the hacker.
Groaning with wrathful eyes and repugnant lullabies,
But to the metropolitans, ere his face a permanent smile lay.
On the concrete stage, stood the robotic man revived
by an assemblage of connoisseur engineers in their stay.
Electric sparks bifurcated into forked lightning and Nanotechnology
awoke him from his guileless-faced sleep.
Brought into the worldly realm shook microchip powered man who assumed the title of a billionaire tracker.

She was a hunted angel- Seraphim that lived in a hominid body who had been discovered online.
Discovered that she had been stalked by a nefarious monster with a calculating brain.
-Beelzebub controlled who wanted this virtuous angel as his gain.
Inhuman with no compassion, unknown to the public's perception and mind.

Into the flame nebula her soul was taken, replaced inside with seraph
W here the hacker stole a glance at her picture,
he hounded her on a gps satellite
For her I lament but under the shadow of the wings.
Of a Morphnus guianensis she hides, with God's light
A test in the macrocosm to show one's valour and strength, against her rights.
Prophecy and wisdom in human flesh sending signals to her whenever he spied.

All the world loved him and most looked at her as their enemy in their ethical philosophy
W alking in war fields in her odyssey,
W ithin a lonely friendless world without a penny.
Summoned to the cherub order at night, he laughed mockingly at her
appearance. The King of the globe with humming birds as his associates that
deceived many.

Breathing embers behind closed doors, being entertained by Jezebel whores
Rather her existence in an asylum, trying to turn her against God in this spiritual
war. W hat a venturesome heart she had, daughter of man without archangel wings.
Pestilence in her ears, conflicting her very cognition, under spells of divination.
Mind control before her computer placed by him, mental stings were a few of the things
And in the name of the gods he believed in, mirror images in the morning before a global nation.

To the sky she's cried at night "Free your damsel," pointing to the Horsehead Nebula.
For earth knows not how to treat her, pleading to the Almighty's illumination so
stellar.
Angry with the attacks of this unsuspicious schemer, in need of an oxygen mask with the Holy Spirit;
The people of the terrestrial sphere were plagued with fear of his power and domination.
At nightfall the counsel of elders, leaders of the unfallen worlds watched her battle where she was stationed.
Voices haunting her sleep, all in the name of technology, laying in her home in safety.

W as she a victim bef ore of an exorcism, cracking toes and fingers?
Levitation in her coma, stigmata, memories and contemplation that
lingered. In this dormancy, to the underworld he went to taunt her
habitually.
Obsessed with her sexually, watching her on satellite, attacking her relentlessly.
Life without privacy in the eyes of Rokossovsky and mentally drained was she.

Spirits roaming the world started attacking her below the twelve tribes of heaven.
W ith tears of acid, he practiced sorcery on her for days and nights, seven times
seven. Extravagant billionaire wearing fluorescent suits and trousers had he been,
A socialite with many escorts at arm until he discovered sweet Calista in the scene.
Her friends deserted her thinking she was schizophrenic and fatuous.
Impossible they'd say beneath the protoplanetary nebulae, condemning as blasphemous.

Blinking lights that moved from left to right in the sky, taunting her knowledge.
Virgins convulsed at her statements, thinking perhaps she belonged settled on the city's pavements.
Distressed at their ignorance, she rode thro' the Scottish forests with her Clydesdale.
Jumping o'er the rivers in the lowlands, shouting "Rescue me sire" meeting a group of shires.
A whirlwind came as she stood in between the horses circling her below the dark dust and
gases. Falling into the company of some Rhododendrons, staying in a village with the loyal
masses.

In the dead of night, he assaulted her chassis in spirit with great force,
Convulsions and tremors opening a thousand doors against Diabolus in the spiritual wars.
Seraphim ascending out of her body with an icicle Szabla from the heavenly source.
Into the mesosphere, bending backwards shooting towards him like Perseids ,
Knocking against the grotesque beast with the head of a lion and hands of
Elapidae.

Roaring like millenaries of Panthera Leones she flew into the ozonosphere crushing his cranium
The universe shook at the blitzkrieg between the two, as Seraph gave her last attack against Apollyon,
Commanding meteoroids that darted like Maserin military daggers toward his way,
And in the speed of light they f ought ensphering the planet in a vortex covering the world in darkness,
The stars bedimming that surrounded them like matrices in an atmosphere already so dull,
Clashing swords like the horns of tempestuous bulls
Defeating this creature with the sum of eighteen while in spiritual exemption.

Body arisen off the Maiden pink terrain gasping for air in a bed of hay,
To the sudden sight of a burning pinewood tree.
Thunderbolt on the crown below watching the dominator of fiends,
W ith eyes of Squamata as hundreds of Cantharidae and Staphylinidae scampered to its feet. A
mouthful of parasitic bees opening slowly dictating orders to capture her by the knees.
Electroconvulsive therapy, she lay in a bed shuddering bef ore a group of anesthesiologists in this
field.

Hurt was she by the abduction in her former youth
At the corner of the ward, flew in a cherub playing a flute
W reathed with cords, destined for quietus and eternal rest.
Ruminations of felo-de-se as a dejected adolescent at the crest.
W eary of therapeutics, she pointed her fingers at the open window
To the night sky, flickering refulgence declaring the satellite.
Cyberpunk grinned that his target without evidence was viewed in a maniacal light.

FOLLOW THE
FASHION

To a world of evolutionary fashion, I held my hands open with a sighting and time compass
Closing one's eyes, speak'st I of chronicles which took one into a world from the past
Inside a canvas of Nattier, danced I with La Camargo being led by Marie-Madeleine Guimard
W earing our romantic tutus, for an ethereal genius of ballet fanning with a group of playing cards
Zephyrs formed phalanges twisting and twirling, bef ore doing the arabesque penchée in the Archduchess's yard

I

Before Marie Antoinette, beneath the fluffy cumuli with her 'robe a la polonaise' as an enchantress
Into an atmosphere of haute couture in Versailles' royal glamour, hoopskirts and whalebone corsets
Heights of fantasy in a setting of aristocracy doing a battement développé as in a painting from Degas
Thrusting Rosa Canina and Rosa Synstylae around while wearing an empire silhouette as a Neo-classic
actress Alluring Mr. and Mrs. W illiam Hallett along with Madame de Pompadour robed in her embroidered gown
Changing one's pace into the Belle Époque in Paris greeting ladies with elaborate parasols curtseying down
Sweet Stradivarius sounds came in a scene of enlightenment and Romanticism,
Dripped with lace to polished prettiness
Pirouetting before the harem girls draped in flowing pantaloons and turbans with vivid colours in the shadowy mist
Spinning with the compass with my oculi closed, in Japan we appear bef ore powder-faced geishas in exotic kimono
And so I meet the men dressed in Hakamas, getas and textured fabrics holding datejimes standing in a row

Holding Aubrieta deltoidea intimately with Jeanne Paquin in Buenos Aires, Madrid and London
Admiring the f ashions of pastel and tailored day dresses, inhaling the air with shimmers of light and fun
Of great significance, we met Jacques Doucet in a galaxy of frills and lace ruffles- the colour of faded flowers
Sipping cups of 'Thés des Poètes Solitaires' from Mariage Frères,
W hile discussing fashion philosophy with the ancient master of fashion design
Speaking words so kind, in the sublime glamour of the night with intentions so benign
Under the moonshine, the compass pointed to Venice to the couture house of Mariano
Fortuny, And swinging one's arms so passionately, spiraling in a tea gown pleated exquisitely.
Hammering one's fists to classical repertoire from a group of Russians playing Tchaikovsky,
Staring at the aqueous reflections of the Venetian lagoon, in the garment that Marie Anne de Cupis de Camargo wore
Gown of finest silk- the Elements of Mexican cochineal, indigo from the Far East and Breton straw

II

A cheerful dance of Charleston and Shimmy meeting the Golden age of fashion in the 1920's
Situated in a party of dresses with long trains to above the knee pinafores as hibiscus keys
W hat zing in the compass wheeling uncontrollably and vibrancy in our adventurous personalities
Feather boas, embroidery, cloche hats, flapper styles and showy accessories.
Inside a room with a Steinway piano playing itself, there stood Gabrielle Bonheur adorned in dozens of Akoya pearls
Delighted at her expensive simplicity, I listened to her fashion philosophy and vogue metaphysics
Consciousness in the decade, smiling at the little black dress, bob hairstyles, jersey knit as one twirls

Saying hello to Jean Patou with style of originality, mixture of luxury and practicality
Taking the position of 'attitude en pointe', like Dudinskaya to his menswear in an increasing mood of informality
Short suit jackets, knickers, tuxedos, heels and swaying into the 1930's with ease
Picking the Kalmia latifolia in a garden of Ericaceae, I whirled in a lobster dress from Elsa Schiaparelli
Posed I as an antique statue, inspiring a timeless and beautiful evening gown outstretching one's arms with glee
O Madeleine Vionnet, how the ladies loved her as they bobbed to the Queen of the bias cut and walking with a strut,
Her garments came to lif e as the chiffon, silk, and Moroccan crepe mingled,
Creating an astonishingly poised and titillating effect, presenting a flowing and elegant line as one tingled.

III

The December twilight romanced the dinner with my companion and I, authorizing fresh winter winds
Our necks covered with handmade printed silk square scarves from Hermès while holding a 'Kelly bag'
W e walked with held hands in this faraway land, our ears tightly devoted to clarinets and C melody saxophone pins
Clutching his body, we did a jitterbug after a few Hemingway Daiquirís when so suddenly, I pirouetted leaving my love behind
Into the arms of Christian Dior I fell in early 1953 in a different society,
Being introduced to the sheer sophistication of style and feminine elegance of his dresses in a fabric sea

Whirling with the compass into a time capsule to another fashion house of the frugal prince of luxury.
What evidence was greater than his apparent individuality and inventiveness to the legendary Cristobal Balenciaga Esagri.
High waisted and chemise dresses underlining his mastery of fashion design,
Celebrated as one of the few couturiers in fashion history at the height of his artistry.

I smiled when I saw Audrey Hepburn tasting Oolong tea gracefully with Jacqueline
Kennedy, Wearing alabaster Betinna blouses from the house of Givency.
It's a wonderful thing to smile in style and as I confess, going through a different door of time
Wandering in a setting with Hollywood designers passing by,
In the 1950's creating fashion allurement for Grace Kelly while savoring Sicilian wine.
I shall fast forward as I sigh, having acknowledged the fashion of the 1960's, 1970's and the
1980's. O birth of mini-skirts dared the legs of women meet from Mary Quant,
And revolutionary yet exquisite tuxedo suits for ethnic models from Yves Saint Laurent.

IV

Three o'clock on a March afternoon, twisting my torso I met Dame Margot Fonteyn
As we performed fouettés en tournant before a group of bell-bottomed hippies sitting at a wall fountain.
The air smelt like deep pink Magnolia blossoms and Classic white gardenia crown jewels on a full moon
And at midnight, she partnered with Rudolf Nureyev as they did in the Kingdom of shades to the Danse de cygnes tune.
Gripping my time compass, in this lunar state I had already said hello to movements of Glam rock,
Broad shouldered designs, Pop-Art inspired jackets in the futuristic universe of Christian Lacroix, in the world of haute couture.
Human Papilionidae draped in the clinging style of Donna Karan and the simple sophistication of Ralph Lauren in the future.

If one were to say, after the dancing and sipping teacups of lovely tea through ages of space
From the days of short skirts made of sweat shirting, leotards, headbands, and leg warmers from Norma Kamali
Phenomenal stilettos strutting the streets and over the knee boots from Manolo Blahnik,
Along with impeccable wild animal print attire, signature patchworks and flowery superfluities from Just Cavalli.
Time transcended into the shower-dress being worn by the best, car dresses from Karl Lagerfeld in the fashion
fest. Speeding in a SSC Ultimate Aero, a fashionista followed the fashion in Gucci with "Jackie O'" as her side kick
Shall I express the latest quest of flamboyant extravagance in Milan and luxurious fabrics from Prada,
While holding a Japanese sandalwood fan being entertained by women in a large display of
Buchaechum. V
Standing at a busy street in the midsummer night stood La Camargo,
Wearing a dazzling red DVF wrap dress, flirting with a gentleman suited in Armani Collezioni from Chicago
His mystery was in his grin as his slow breaths caressed the air, clutching her body beneath the nebulae
Staring into the spinning time compass, we disappeared through another door inhaling winter whiffs on a frigid day.
Converses with a crowd of denizens attired in black sheered mink furs from the house of
Posen, Being taken to an ice château by a pack of snow wolves from Alaska that had been
chosen.
Tenebrous morning brought shouts from strangers in the distance warmly dressed in LV leopard fur threads
I suppose their fuzzy heads were ready to sleep in permafrost igloo beds.
And in my bungalow I lay with my time compass in my hands after visiting various lands
To seize every memory, holding them dear to my heart whilst having accepted that we had to part.

BUBO SCANDIACUS

My feathered friend from the frigid Antarctican end,
Sitting on a cirrus cloud in the *Terra Australis* posing wondering when,
My dear feathered friend Armstrong née Stockholm
With his black and white feathers shall depart into the skies and roam.

Dotted yellow eyes searching the icy lands dressed in his daily best
Replenishing his every breath, waving his heroic sovereign wings
Here I stand patiently on a polar ice cap, awaiting his return in the sombre winter's quest
Taking the form of a seaplane, his growth extended into one of the greatest kings
To collect me from danger with Ptolemy on his back flying along with his family Strigidae
As he lifts me off my feet in brumal sleep in this resolution and adventure on this special day.

Searching the South Pole on the harf ang's wings I fly o'er the Vinson Massif
Frostbitten hands taking charge gliding in the distance toward remnants of Gondwana
Into a land of emperor penguins with elaborate eyelashes through the Aurora Australis
A postcard scene, against the strong kabatic winds sat our fantasy glacier fortress on Lake Vostok
Heartwarming waves of Colobanthus quitensis on display before fireworks of Sigma Octantis

Thrilling optical phenomenons and charming illusions of bliss
Spins in a wildly fanciful Apocalypse in versatile winter's kiss
Krek Krek, prek prek my hooting owl goes proudly holding his thick plumage
In an austere fashion beneath Jupiter's moon we danced before Europa's southern cage
Mesmerized so deeply thrown, we witnessed a cataclysmal avalanche from the Pacific Ring of Fire
Fictions of Mount Erebus's mighty mouth, on Armstrong's back fleeing the phonotephrite lava flows enraged.

Fleeing on this chaotic stage, o'er anorthoclase crystals in a solar eclipse Commander and
leader of the iceberg armies beneath Mount Terror's furious lips Phantasmagoria slumbering in
a community of cirrocumuli castellanus with my bubo scandiacus Fantasies and deathless
romances in an ocean of permafrost diamonds through nature's fuss Galloping in the open air as
fearless naginatas in a battle of Samurai away from snowy waterfalls Hovering on his wings
covering the alkaline waters,
As two-dimensional silhouettes overlooking an earthly baptism of ice.

Saluting our audiences of Aptenodytes forsteri wearing coronals of heat
Landing safely on a frigid board of dominoes on the East Antarctic Ice
Sheet. Opening his eyes widely like French rococo bracket clocks seeking
eternity, Meritorious of adoration, chasing lemmings and hopes of frozen
immortality.
Spreaded arms like Commerson's dolphin flippers on moving ice opposing daylight's vice.

Acrobats at the Cirque Fernando in an oil painting of Renoir,
On centennial time scales of epic aftermath opening doors of new beginnings
Quivering in wintertide's beastly embrace, blowing puffs of nipping air in our adventure's convex face
Imperishable truths of our inextinguishable flames as trusted friends taking flight in the scene of snowy white's haste.
Into the frosty wilderness, carried like a phosphorescent package toward his nest of edacious owlets.

Pennons curved in the form of a V, spinning as a polar vortex blanketing my body's skin
Undresses his feather suit draping me with crafty gloved hands sheltering from the weather's windy tin whistles
Fitful bursts of energy from the sinister gelidness as his physique desireth summery kilts,
Responding to an assemblage of astrophysicists making cacophonous booms from
pistols.

Visions in the twilight of stellar dynamics and foamy textures of galaxy globular clusters
Pointing whilst analyzing through magnetohydrodynamics the empyrean Hubble flows
On a flocculent cloud rested Michael Faraday awaiting his safeguard from Stockholm's heroic flurries
As the milieu played tricks on his cognizance, disappearing in an electric flash without any worries.

THE KISS

Symmetrically, swinging romantically in quintessential Tuscany
It wasn't much of a mystery to see, in this esoteric philosophy
 when two people were in love.
In a setting of enamoring Columbidae and dahlia apple blossoms
 beduffled by calmative breezes, flew chiliads of Barbary doves.
Phantasmagoric hills bejeweled with cypress trees
 beneath stratocumuli castellanus filled with polyfloral honey.
Into a kaleidoscopic sphere of delineations and variegated geometric prisms,
the demure lady covered her dithering shoulders as his embracing lips
 met the evening's crepuscular charm.

 Lo! As barefooted dreamers spiraling in the zygomorphic equation,
 predilections of pupils dilating
Fervent kiss as Rodin's sculpture with passionate trembling of his emphatic jaw,
After pluvious sundowns of contemptuous calignosities imperturbably waiting.
A pair of Agapornis lilianae in lover's land with infinite bliss,
 osculating love's unfeigned kiss in their tryst of mating,
Spinning as in the Pegasus Dwarf Spheroidal opening a Rafflesia arnoldii knobbed door.
Tis' a burning prayer of igneous desire whither they wander sweet Adalvino and Callidora.

Rich in promise,their hearts aligned as he bestows
 his merry blithesome message on her lips
Hearts beating to the zephyr's canzonet with soul and body
 holding her vestal hips.
Francouzský polibek, kielisuudelma, thola maranawa
 in a field of comatose Madagascar jasmine flowers Cavorting fervidly, relaxed by the ambiance's
intimacy at love's boiling point on a Galilean thermometer, In a state of affinity sniffing each other's
nostrils fondly through cosmic powers.

And one astonishing night in the quintessence of their delectation,
Under the luminescence of visiting Ganymede,their mesmerized faces rubbed in the macrocosm's station.
Embracing her bent body like a wooden mannequin figure, he cuddled in his dream's primeval
rhythms, Along bubbles of sagacity perforating to vociferations of covetous convocations.
Treasured notion of love on a vignette from Leibniz whilst observing beatific wisdoms.

O mother of the senses, to touch her cushiony vulnerable palms
And share delectable kisses with sudden jerks
'Shudder to intellectualize', unhurriedly closing their eyes amidst their intense desideratum where the wind lurks
Sublime emotions launching into metagalactic space in this empyreal ocean of emptiness on a logarithmic spiral beach.
Noumenon and phenomenon of the greatest kiss to venerated morning's sun-staggering jewels in a triumphant speech.
Magnetic shocks stimulating Sardanapalian intuition between gentleman and butterfly against life's malignant
pessimism.

Conciliating mordant throngs, running toward the fortress there
 stood bondservants hitting feng gongs
In an antechamber where Michelangelo, Sandro Botticelli
Galileo Galilei, Amerigo Vespucci and Puccini sat.
Reverberant merriment among the covey whose fervour for music granted exuberance whilst fixating with scissors-
glasses. But tonight they flee to the Renaissance hills in Radicof ani to a Neptunian sea of adventurous snowflake obsidian.
To redeem the power of their astonishing last kiss of chivalrous reputation and prepotent over sentimental soap operas.

Der Kuss in the erudition of the Golden period, 'twas an invigorating innervation
And faintly in a courtyard of shimmering, extravagant Cassiterites and quartz crystals,
They wander as a pair of Meander Prepona butterflies morphing into a doublet of Aegidienbergers in the Italian nation.
Visages slowly looking away, they press their slim fingers against each other's lips advancing epicurean nestles in an elemen t
so mystical
Releasing entanglements of the mind in the cosmos remarkably unkind but deeply they are in love with poetic tears that trickle.

THE FASHIONISTA

Fair lady strutted herself as a luminary that she hath not been.
For those were the reverberations of envious and jaundiced haters.
Her f abricated modish coat of Florentine leather
with Acinonyx jubatus print hath covered her sun-kissed skin.
The prima donna's title is fashionista denizens, a rosso corsa neckerchief
and a momentous hint.
Holding tickets dear to their hearts, she gave her walk before the crowd
of soothers with affable eyes and a sharp squint.

The response to the cynic philosophers of this gentlewoman is an incandescent smile.
As her instinctive poses graced kodachromes, microfilm and magazines issuing her
style.
O how far and wide with stride, she was chronicled due to her modality and her kit.
In the director's first scene twirled her physique, so sleek in the thespian caper
All the world's a game so play it', which were some words in the skit.
Many acknowledgements and conferments to the dame, rocking with every whim.

The helmer whistled with affirmation that her sashay was just right.
Her admirers observe as she winks fluttering her eyelashes whilst uttering to the chaps not to fight.
Fashionista blues was the soprano aria that she sang.
O and to the waves of innovation, into her moon box she laughed and fashionably late while the handbell
rang! She curtsied before her cohort of onlookers who joined in her fashionista gang.
Be good to the Renaissance woman with lengthen'd lif e on the accentuated motherland.

There's another detail about the fashionista one ought to know.
She did not emerge over night, as it took time for her to design her show.
And one ought to understand that this personage is one of the f airest in the
land. O so fair, you may see her driving her buggati veyron alongside a ferrari
enzo
Or as a socialite wassailing Chateau Lafitteis with her entourage in Montenegro.

Tanzanite heels, Cinderella slippers and Retro Rose Stilettos
Are those f ound in her wardrobe closet along with faddish clothes in
rows And such, at instances turning heads in her daily life, some as
wives Rhapsodic, in awe and in entrancement are their f ans from various
lands.

Fashionista, f ashionista, there's no one like the fashionista.
There's not another tellurian around with such strength f or the cosmos know her as a role mod el.
Marie Antoinette is her icon and they declare that her flawless makeup came from a revolutionary
bottle. W hat's this bottle of mystery and Rosette Nebula that glistened on her face as a binary star?
Stellar Winds and interstellar clouds from foreign lands with supernova explosions in galaxies af ar.
The radiation from the stars excite the atoms in the nebula and this defines the world of a fashionista.